Master Class

Master Class

WITH TOBA GARRETT

Cake Artistry and Advanced Decorating Techniques

PHOTOGRAPHS BY **Lucy Schaeffer**

ILLUSTRATIONS BY **Christine Mathews**

WILEY

Copyright © 2013 by Toba Garrett. All rights reserved.

Published by John Wiley & Sons, Inc., Hoboken, New Jersey.

Published simultaneously in Canada.

LIBRARY OF CONGRESS CATALOGING-IN-PUBLICATION DATA
Garrett, Toba.
Master class with Toba Garrett: cake artistry and advanced decorating techniques / Toba Garrett; photographs by Lucy Schaeffer; illustrations by Christine Mathews.
Includes index.
Description based on print version record and CIP data provided by publisher; resource not viewed.
ISBN 978-0-470-58122-3 (cloth) – 1. Cake decorating. 2. Cake. I. Title.
TX771.2
641.86'539–dc23
2012018528

Printed in China

10 9 8 7 6 5 4 3 2 1

. . . to our Wendy,
with love and a lifetime of memories

CONTENTS

Acknowledgments   viii

Preface   ix

INTRODUCTION TO CAKE ARTISTRY   1

THE ESSENTIALS   7

THE CAKE DESIGNS   33

ANNIVERSARY CAKES   35

BIRTHDAY CAKES   57

GROOM'S CAKES   83

WEDDING CAKES   105

SEASONAL CAKES   125

SMALL BITES:
DECORATED COOKIES AND CUPCAKES   149

THE RECIPES   165

Appendix   204

Index   220

ACKNOWLEDGMENTS

I would like to thank the many individuals that worked so hard in making this book a reality. First, my Wiley family headed by my editors Christine McKnight and Mary Cassells, who have successfully guided me in my third project. I can't thank them enough for the hard work and dedication that they have provided me over the years. Also to Marina Padakis Lowry, senior production editor; Alison Lew and Gary Philo at Vertigo Design NYC; and Leah Stewart, copy editor. And I would also like to thank Rachel Livsey for suggesting the title. I would also like to graciously thank Lucy Schaeffer, my photographer; Christine Mathews, my illustrator; Patty Laspia, my chief assistant; Rashawn Robinson, my assistant; Shane Walsh, Lucy Schaeffer's assistant; and Martha Bernabe, prop stylist.

I would also like to thank my colleagues at the Institute of Culinary Education for their continued support and my many students over the past few decades. They have taught me as much as I have imparted my knowledge and wisdom to them. I thank them for sharing their many stories and cultures with me.

To my many friends and colleagues in the cake decorating world, I thank you. You are too many to name, but remember that you are always in my thoughts and prayers. Thank you for the years of camaraderie and true sharing and support.

Special thanks to my husband and lifelong partner, James, for his undying love and for being a true champion of all of my causes. To our beloved son, Phoenix, and all our family members, I thank you all.

Finally, I thank and have deeply missed Wendy Lipkind Black, my literary agent.

PREFACE

This book explores my personal and creative artistry—the cake decorating techniques and styles that I hold dear and that have brought me to the attention of my peers and furthered my career over the past three decades.

Some of the cake designs in this book are inspired by everyday life and the people and places around me, and some are personal remembrances of my travels and teaching. In my travels, I try to look at new places with an artistic eye and see how I can incorporate those ideas into a cake design. Inspiration can come from many sources—from the color of a house, the stonework on a street, or the engravings and relief work on churches or monuments; to the simplicity of the blue-green waters of the sea or the humility, honesty, and patriotism of the people in a particular place. I have also been influenced by the food I have eaten and the pride that each country takes in its cuisine. Food tells you the essence of a people. Foods as simple as a pasta sauce full of flavor from tomatoes grown in someone's backyard and the tastiest roasted and salted sardines I have ever eaten have provided insight into the culture and traditions of the places I've visited. I am, of course, inspired by some of the desserts I have enjoyed in countries around the world, from the local traditions of the Philippines, Brazil, and Portugal to the exquisite and elegant creations I have enjoyed in France and in Italy. My newest venture is New Zealand, where I am finishing the writing of this book. I have immensely enjoyed their chocolate mud and fruitcakes, as well as their wines, olive oil, and gigantic mussels.

Each cake design in this book takes me back to a moment in time or a new experience that I humbly share with you, the reader. I hope you will enjoy some of the cake art and recipes and feel the inspiration that I have felt.

I hope this book will encourage you to explore the hidden depths of your imagination and allow yourself to create exciting designs in cake artistry. This book is simply a springboard to the infinite ideas that can be achieved— ideas and possibilities we haven't even tapped into yet. What seemed so impossible to do decades ago is now a technique that can be learned quickly. Use your surroundings, your culture, or anything that challenges your ability to go beyond recognized techniques. Create your own uniqueness and add to a growing industry that's electrified by the art of cake decorating.

INTRODUCTION TO CAKE ARTISTRY

From inspiration to design

Inspiration is all around you, from nature to fashion to architecture. Even something as simple as where you live can be a starting point in translating inspiration into a creative design. As an example, a New York City prewar apartment, built around 1917, with raised moldings, arches, perpendicular lines, pastel walls, hardwood flooring, and French glass doors could spark the creative process.

As a cake artist, I would take that spark of inspiration and envision a cake in the shape of a building, a church, or a monument. The 90-degree angles of the apartment would guide my creative vision and help inform which techniques and styles I would use. For example, I might choose to create an architectural cake with three-dimensional raised pipework and pillars, rather than a soft, rounded design with smooth edges, ruffles, and dainty touches.

If you feel that you lack creativity and you struggle to come up with design concepts of your own, you can do what most of us did when we first started—that is, take inspiration from someone else and then add your own touches to that inspiration. For example, to pursue the architectural concept described above, I would look at examples of the English and South African–style technique known as "Nirvana." This is a beautiful style of work that is very architectural. The cakes are generally hexagonal or octagonal in shape, with lots of 90-degree angles, raised lines, and panels of flooded collars in pastel tones.

You could take this entire concept and use it as the starting point for your own cake. Then you might adapt the concept by changing the shape of the cake and the size and shape of the collars, adding overpiped lines to represent the raised moldings in the apartment, and adding some pipework or collars in the shape of arches.

Another source of inspiration from the prewar apartment could be Joseph Lambeth's works on classical or late-Victorian-era cake artistry. Lambeth created a plethora of designs that include three-dimensional pipework, cushion lattice, raised and dimensional pipework, bias relief, flood work, works in the shape of rotundas with pillars, pipework, and molds in the shape of scrolls or cameos, and lots and lots of freehand molding and piping. As with the Nirvana style, you could pull one or two aspects from Lambeth's work to spark your creative process, and then add your own ideas to make it your own.

You don't have to go far for inspiration. Look to color, texture, lines, the landscape, or the mood of the city right outside your front door to start the creative process.

The design process

Putting things down on paper is the most difficult task for most cake artists. The first thing many beginning cake artists say is "I can't draw." But you don't have to be a skilled artist to put down an idea on paper. A #2 pencil, a sketch pad and a big fat eraser are all you need to begin the process of designing a cake.

First, begin "sketching," using only the small eraser at the end of your pencil. If you're drawing a circle or a square to start your design, it's easier and more forgiving to begin by using an eraser. Modify the eraser design until you have a circle or a square that looks the way you intended, and then trace over the eraser drawing with the pencil. Alternatively, you can use Microsoft Word to create the initial shapes for your cake design. To do this, open a new Word document and select the "Insert" menu. From the "Basic Shapes" feature, click on either the "can" shape for a round or oval-shaped cake tier, or the "cube" shape for a square or rectangular tier. Once the cursor appears on your screen, move it to the right to stretch the top of the shape and then move down to enlarge it. Now, the can or cube looks like a cake tier. Then create another can or cube shape, enlarge it to resemble a larger tier, and move the first tier on top of the second. You will now have a drawing of a two-tiered cake that you can print to paper and use as a starting point for your cake design.

Next, it's time to add decorative elements to the sketch to dress up the cake design. In my wedding cake workshops in New York City, I encourage students who say they cannot draw to simply use basic shapes to represent each element on the cake. For example, you might draw circles to represent roses on a cake, and curves between the circles to represent leaves. I also bring books and magazines to my workshops for inspiration, and have students mimic what they see, or trace or transfer a design from a book to their drawings. When the drawing starts to take shape, I can see the light in my students' eyes. As they become more confident in their abilities, it becomes easier and easier for them to add to their drawings to make their cake designs truly special.

I would also encourage you to use colored pencils to add shading to your initial sketches. This adds dimension to your work and can help provide greater insight into the final cake design. It is also a good idea to make several different sketches of the same project, with different elements in each drawing, to provide you with a range of options for the finished design. One of the drawings should be more simplistic; something that can be executed with little effort. The others can include more challenging techniques, though any design element you include in your sketches should be realistic within your skill set.

Often, a design idea will change as you move from the drawing to the actual project. Your first drawings should contain your initial thoughts, and then should be modified and refined as you continue to develop the simple sketches into a working idea. You might find that your initial thoughts aren't practical or are more difficult to execute than you anticipated. On the other hand, you may find that you can expand on the design and add more elements as your confidence grows.

Achieving mastery

As with any art, mastering a full range of cake artistry techniques can take a lifetime. Some basic techniques are relatively easy and can be learned and mastered within months, as long as you practice often. Other techniques require skill, patience, great hand-eye coordination, and truly serious study in order to master. Anyone seeking to achieve mastery in cake artistry should begin by perfecting the foundational techniques listed below. Many of these are covered in "The Essentials" chapter (see pages 7–31), but for a complete guide to the fundamentals of cake decorating, you may also wish to consult an introductory cake decorating guide, such as my book *Professional Cake Decorating*, Second Edition.

PIPING

This is perhaps the most important skill in cake artistry. Creating beautiful designs through piping is truly an art. Piping should be the first skill a novice cake decorator perfects, but often it is not. Today, it is fairly easy to make a cake look amazing using rolled fondant cutouts, molds, lace design presses, and a relatively new electric cutting machine called the Cricut—all with little to no skill involved. To the average observer, a cake made using these techniques might look like the work of a talented cake artist, but that is far from the truth. Used in tiny doses, these techniques can add more depth to a cake design, but the foundation of any good cake design should, in most cases, be based on fine pipework, which is one of the most difficult techniques to perfect and which adds a whole different level of mastery to a cake.

Starting with the basics of buttercream or royal icing pipework, every cake decorator should be proficient in all types of cake border skills, such as classic and large shells, e-shells, curved shells with shell accents, zigzags, rosettes, reverse shells, ropes, and garlands. Side designs such as fleur-de-lis with drop strings, ruffles, swags, scrolls, and lattice are also essential, and these are just the basics. Floral piping, including rosebuds, half-roses, and full-blown roses; cherry, apple, peach, and orange blossoms; and violets, sweet peas, pansies, and daisies are also essential skills for every cake artist. And of course, writing on cakes is another foundational technique that requires skills in calligraphy or a beautiful writing hand.

Then there is the art of royal icing pipework, which includes filigree, advanced scroll piping, cushion lattice, stringwork, lacework, cornelli lace, sotas, flooding, brush embroidery, freehand embroidery, overpiping, and many more related skills. These techniques alone can take years to master.

I would advise every decorator to begin his or her training by mastering all of the buttercream piping skills, and then learning a few techniques in the royal icing skills category. Little by little, you can then build on this foundation by adding additional techniques to what you have already learned in order to build a portfolio of sound and professional techniques.

ROLLED FONDANT AND GUMPASTE

Rolled fondant and gumpaste techniques can be just as important as pipework in cake artistry, but should be used in appropriate dosages. These skills are easier to learn than piping skills, and a rolled fondant cake covered in beautiful gumpaste flowers may appear easy, but skills such as making gumpaste flowers can still take years of practice to perfect. The more skill you have, the more realistic the flowers will look. When you incorporate color appropriately, which is an important skill all on its own, as well as floral arranging skills, you will see your mastery beginning to develop. I often encourage my students to take a course in fresh and dry floral arranging at a local art school or botanical garden. These classes teach a variety of arranging skills, from large bouquets to corsages, which can then be applied when arranging gumpaste flowers.

There are also many pastry skills used by cake artists that should be practiced and perfected, such as chocolate work, pulled and blown sugarwork, pastillage, and last but not least, the art of baking. Flavor first!

Great baking skills are no longer something that a cake artist can ignore. In the distant past, a cake decorator did not have to have strong baking skills in order to be successful. But today, while decorating and baking are still separate entities, each is essential when creating a cake for a client or for family and friends. As clients' palates become increasingly sophisticated, cake artists can no longer get away with using prepared cake mixes. I recommend taking a course in baking skills that includes different methods of cake preparation, as well as compiling a collection of great cake and icing recipes. It is essential that your cakes taste as good as they look, and baking and icing skills can require as much practice and refinement as the techniques you will use for decorating the cake!

How to use this book

This book is divided into three main chapters. First is The Essentials. This chapter is a review of the foundational techniques needed to execute the designs in this book. You should diligently review all of these essential techniques first, before executing any of the designs in the book. A good overview of the basics will make the decorating process less stressful and will give you some ammunition when tackling the cake designs.

The second and largest chapter of the book includes the cake designs. These are fun, yet tricky. Some require a lot of preparation and a variety of skills to execute, while others are simpler and more streamlined. These designs combine many of the skills covered in The Essentials chapter with some more specialized and advanced techniques.

Some of the designs are quite technical, and require a certain amount of precision in order to execute. The Nirvana Cake, the Oriental Stringwork Cake, the Crescents and Scroll Cake, and the Australian Stringwork Cake, for example, each have a specific approach with precise techniques and guidelines to follow. As the cake artist, you can alter those rules and mix and match techniques to create your own designs, but it is important to stay true to the essence of the style. The rest of the cake designs in the book are a bit less technical and offer the cake artist more flexibility. Each of the designs in this book is based on my own personality and style of cake artistry, but with a bit of imagination and a strong skill set, you can adapt and adjust each one to fit your own style.

Last, but certainly not least, are the recipes. No cake design would be complete without a plethora of recipes to choose from to help complement the cake design. For each of the cake designs in this book, I have suggested a cake recipe, as well as a complementary icing and, in some cases, a filling. These flavors are not etched in stone. As the cake artist, it is often your job to suggest to the client what cake would best complement the design. Often, clients will come to you with cake suggestions, or they may ask you for options to choose from.

It is also important to have a variety of cake recipes on hand because often, clients will come to a cake artist with questions or concerns about the cake and the ingredients used. There are many individuals today who are allergic to wheat, nuts, corn, dairy, and other ingredients, for example. These are issues that all cake artists now face. In some cases, you may be able to meet some of these special needs by simply suggesting an alternate cake recipe. In other cases, addressing special dietary needs will require revamping the entire recipe. With experimentation, for example, some of the cake recipes can be made gluten-free by replacing the cake flour with a gluten-free flour, such as potato flour, vital gluten-free flour, or multi-blend gluten-free flour. These changes won't exactly replicate the original flavor and texture of the cake, but they do provide an option for those who can't have wheat.

I invite you to use this book as a stepping stone to your own creative process. Mix and match the designs as you see fit, and remember that in essence, even the most elaborate wedding cake is just a cake with a lot of fuss!

Enjoy!

THE
ESSENTIALS

The skills in this section are necessary to execute many of the cake designs in this book. Although many of these skills may already be familiar to you, perfecting them is key to giving your cakes that tailored and polished look. Many of these techniques can be used independently, but some can also be combined together to give your cake an exquisite look.

Cornelli lace

Cornelli lace is one of the easiest forms of embroidery piping. It is not organized like freehand embroidery or brush embroidery. In essence, a PME #0 round tip is dragged to the surface of the cake at a 45° angle and moved in one continuous loose curve. If the cake is iced in buttercream, the tip is held just slightly above the cake's surface and the same technique applied. The finished design looks like one continuous line in tiny small curves that do not intersect.

1. In order to complete this exercise, you will need to ice a cake in rolled fondant, royal icing, or marzipan. Load a medium-size paper cone with 1 Tbsp (14 g) of royal icing and the PME #0 round tip.

2. Position the tip at a 45° angle, if piping on top of the cake, and at a 90° angle if piping on the sides of the cake. With steady pressure, squeeze the bag and move the tip in small curves, slightly scratching the surface of the cake. The curves should be random and never cross each other.

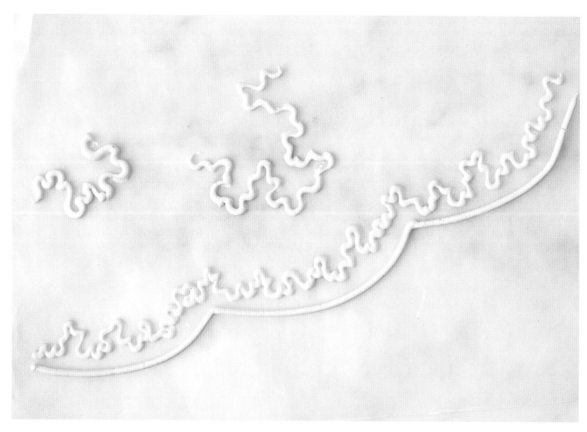

Freehand cornelli lace and cornelli lace in a scalloped design.

Freehand embroidery

Freehand embroidery consists of dots, circles, curves, ovals, quotation marks, commas, and so on. All or some of these marks are organized into a pattern that forms beautiful embroidery that is the hallmark of Australian cake piping. Only in Australia are dots, curves, circles, and so forth organized into dazzling displays of piping artistry.

First, mark the cake into sections that reflect the pattern you wish to use. (See photo below for examples.) Note the center point of the design. The pattern will be mirrored on each side of the center point—that is, whatever you pipe on the left side of the center point you will also pipe on the right. If you are uncomfortable piping freehand onto a finished cake, trace the pattern on see-through paper. Place the pattern on the cake and pinprick the design onto it. Then remove the pattern and pipe over the pinpricked pattern. This is an acceptable technique that allows you to execute accurate designs until you master freehand piping.

1. Trace the pattern onto see-through paper. Tracing the pattern will give you a sense of the placement of the organized dots, circles, curves, and commas.

2. Place 1 Tbsp (14 g) of royal icing in one of the medium-size paper cones with the PME #0 round tip. Transfer the pattern from the see-through paper onto a cake using the pinprick design transfer method. To use this method, trace the pattern onto see-through paper. Place the pattern directly onto an iced cake. Transfer the pattern using a stickpin, making sure that you

Examples of freehand embroidery.

9

keep the pinpricks close together to get a good likeness. Remove the pattern from the cake to reveal the transfer. Transferring the pattern in this exercise will give you good control and a sense of immediate gratification.

3. Piping begins at the center of the pattern and moves from left to right. Pipe directly over the transfer so that you know exactly where to place the circles, ovals, dots, and curves. Slightly drag the tip to the cake's surface when piping the embroidery. Remember to apply light pressure with the PME #0 tip when piping freehand embroidery.

4. Once the pattern is complete, repeat the exercise freehand on another section of the cake, without transferring the pattern to the cake. Look at the traced pattern and copy the pattern by sight onto another section of the cake. Remember, start at the center of the pattern and carefully work from left to right. Continue to practice freehand to become more comfortable with the technique.

Plunger flowers

Plunger flowers, or small blossoms, are basic to the work of busy decorators and pastry chefs. They are easy to make, and they can be made in advance and in an abundance of colors to match any cake. They can be kept for months, or even years, if packaged in a cardboard box and stored in a dry place.

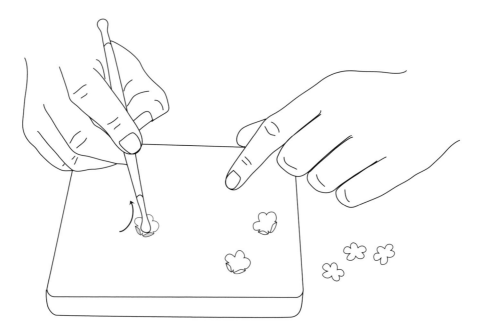

To thin the edge of the petals and cup the flower, pull the dogbone tool from the petal's edge toward the center.

1. Color 3 oz (85 g) of gumpaste as desired or leave it the natural color. Rub a tiny amount of vegetable shortening onto the work surface and roll out the paste with a small nonstick rolling pin until it is petal thin. Transfer the paste to a surface lightly dusted with cornstarch.

2. Press a plunger cutter into the paste and move it back and forth to separate the petals from the rest of the paste. When you lift the cutter, the petals will be attached to it. Place the cutter on a cell pad and press the plunger to release the cupped petals. Repeat this until you have made as many florets as necessary.

3. Position the small ball of a dogbone tool at the edge of one of the blossoms. Gently pull the ball tool toward the center of the flower. This thins the edge of the petal and further cups the flower. Go to the next petal and repeat the technique. Continue until the entire flower is complete.

4. To finish the flower, load a small paper cone with 1 oz (28 g) royal icing and a PME #0 tip, and pipe a small dot of royal icing in the center of each flower.

Freehand drapery

Freehand drapery is not as structured as classical drapery, but it is equally beautiful. A large piece of paste is cut and formed by hand and then each end is pleated into ½-in (1.3-cm) sections and is added to an iced cake in a free-form style. The results are breathtaking!

1. Knead 8 oz (228 g) of fondant or modeling paste until it is pliable. Sprinkle the work surface lightly with cornstarch and roll out the paste into a rectangle, about 6 x 9 in (15.2 x 22.9 cm) and ⅛ in (3 mm) thick. Use an X-acto knife to help cut it to size.

2. Using a pastry brush and a little water, brush the area of the cake where the drapery will be placed. Fold under the top and bottom edges of the paste, about ½ in (1.3 cm) in to form a finished edge of your drape. Then, gather one end of the drape by pleating the drape into ½-in (1.3-cm) folds. Repeat this for the other end of the drape.

3. Place both thumbs at the bottom of the tucked paste, the index fingers at the midpoint, and the middle fingers at the top edge. Gently pick up the paste and move it up and down until it drapes. Carefully attach the drape to the damp area on the cake. Taper the ends of the paste and tear off any excess.

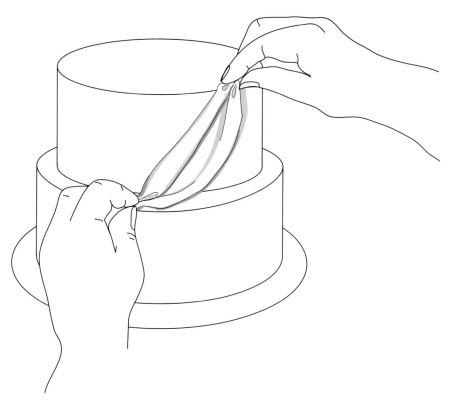

Freehand drapery can be shaped in any way you choose and attached to a wet area of the cake.

4. Make another freehand drape with the remaining fondant and attach it to the cake.

Classical drapery

Classical drapery is more structured than freehand drapery. It requires you to measure your cake before cutting strips of modeling paste or gumpaste, sandwiching the pastes together, and layering the paste to form a pleated look.

1. Rub a little vegetable shortening on the work surface. Roll out 4 oz (114 g) of fondant or modeling paste on the shortening, which helps the fondant adhere to the surface and allows the paste to be rolled thin. The shortening also keeps the fondant intact and stable when strips are cut.

2. Roll and trim the fondant to a rectangle about ⅛ in (3 mm) thick. Cut the rectangle into two or three strips, about 1½ x 6 in (3.8 x 15.2 cm). Turn the strips over and brush the bottom of each with a little egg white. Fold the dry side of each strip to the wet side, developing a pillow or gathered effect.

3. Brush a little egg white on one of the folded strips, just above the seam. Place another folded strip on the wet seam. Brush egg white on the seam of the second folded strip and add the third.

4. Wet the area of the cake where the drapery will appear with water. Carefully pick up the three folded strips by the ends. Shape the strips to the wet surface on the cake. Break off any extended pieces with your fingers and secure the ends of the folded strips to the cake.

5. Make three more folded strips and attach them to the cake where the last three strips ended. The drapery should have a curved or crescent-shaped appearance. Continue adding drapery around the rest of the cake.

Fold each strip of fondant over and attach the strips together to create a gathered effect.

Tassels

Tassels give a textured and Victorian-type look to a cake. These are easily created by using a clay gun fitted with a multi-hole disk and rolled fondant in the desired shade.

1. Knead about 1 oz (28 g) of gold-colored rolled fondant with a little vegetable shortening. Shape it into a 2-in (5.1-cm) log. Place the log into a clay gun fitted with a wire-mesh multi-hole disk.

2. Place the plunger into the gun and apply a lot of pressure as the spaghetti-like strings start to emerge from the gun. Continue to squeeze until about 1½ in (5.1 cm) of paste emerges from the gun. Cut with an X-acto knife. Continue with the same technique to make more tassels.

Cut the tassel from the clay gun with an X-acto knife.

Rope

Rope is a beautiful technique that can also be used in coordination with tassels or braiding.

1. Measure out ½ oz (14 g) of colored gumpaste and knead a tiny amount of vegetable shortening into the paste.

2. Roll the paste into a 3-in (7.6-cm) log and place the log into the barrel of a clay gun. Attach the three-petal disk into the base of the clay gun. Attach the plunger on top and begin to push the plunger. A strand of paste should expel from the gun. Continue until the plunger has met the top of the clay gun and all of the paste has been expelled from the gun. Cut off the paste with an X-acto knife.

3. Hold the strand at both ends and begin to twist the strand in opposite directions to form a rope.

Brush embroidery

Brush embroidery resembles the fine embroidery seen on table linens and napkins. Just as the raised and flat stitching gives lushness to linens, brush embroidery piping adds elegance and style to any cake with a rolled iced surface. With practice, brush embroidery is much easier to do than it looks. A floral design is transferred directly to the cake's surface with a stickpin or to a rolled iced plaque or plain cardboard. In the case of a plaque or cardboard, the design can be transferred using the carbon copy method.

1. To transfer the embroidery design to a cake or plaque using a stickpin, trace the pattern onto a piece of parchment paper or see-through paper. Place the traced pattern on the cake or plaque and secure the ends with masking tape. Transfer the pattern to the cake or plaque by outlining it with a stickpin. Be sure the pinpricks are close together to reveal a good likeness of the pattern. Remove the pattern from the cake or plaque.

    To transfer the design to a gumpaste or marzipan plaque using the carbon copy method, trace the pattern onto see-through paper. Turn the paper over and retrace the pattern in reverse onto a piece of parchment paper. Then reverse the parchment to the right side, place it over the plaque, and carefully tape it in place with masking tape. Retrace the pattern and remove.

2. Once the design is transferred, load one medium-size paper cone with a #2 or #3 round tip and 2 Tbsp (28 g) of royal icing. Start from the outside of the pattern and work your way toward the center of the pattern.

3. Outline the border of one small section of the pattern—for example, one leaf or flower petal—by slightly dragging the tip to the surface. Before the outline dries, dip a #1 or #3 sable paintbrush in a little egg white and carefully brush some of the outline icing toward the center of that section. Use long strokes to lightly brush a thin layer of icing over the entire section of the design. The background should be visible through the layer. Continue to dip the brush in egg white and brush the outline icing, leaving the bulk of the outline icing intact.

4. Continue with the rest of the design, brushing one small section at a time. Let each section dry before beginning the next.

5. When the design is dry, you can use a second paper cone with a PME #0 round tip loaded with 1 Tbsp (14 g) of royal icing to pipe on additional details, such as veins and stems for leaves. Drag the tip slightly to pipe these additional details.

Outline each section of the design and brush the icing in toward the center of each petal and leaf.

Flooding/runouts

This is one of the easiest and most versatile techniques in the art of cake decorating. The decorator outlines a traced image that is covered with plastic wrap and uses a medium-stiff icing. The outline icing is thinned with a little water or pasteurized egg white and placed in a paper cone or a squeeze bottle. The tip of the bottle is placed in the center of the outlined design and pressure is applied to the bottle to release the soft icing. The bottle is then lifted from the surface and a toothpick or paintbrush is used to move it to the perimeter of the design. Once outlined and flooded, the design is air-dried for 2 to 24 hours. The design is then carefully removed from the plastic wrap and placed on a plaque, rolled iced cake, or iced cookie.

This technique can be used to create beautiful monograms, colorful characters, and writing transfer designs.

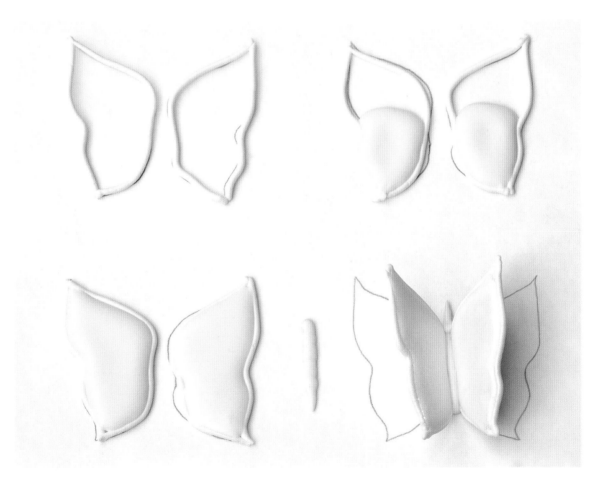

TOP: *Outlining a pattern and beginning to flood the outline.*
BOTTOM: *A fully flooded pattern and an assembled flooded butterfly.*

1. Load 1 oz (28 g) of royal icing in a small or medium-size paper cone fitted with the #2 or #3 round tip. This will be used to outline the runouts. Fill another medium paper cone or small squeeze bottle (with a cover and a small opening at the top) with 4 to 5 oz (114 to 140 g) of flood icing. Place the pattern on a cardboard round or square and tape the ends. Cover the pattern tightly with plastic wrap and secure the ends with masking tape.

2. Position the tip at a 45° angle to the pattern and trace it with the tip just barely above the surface. If outlining a large monogram or a pattern with long lines or curves, touch the pattern surface with the tip and then raise it about 1 in (2.5 cm) above the surface, letting the icing fall to the pattern.

3. To fill in the outline, position the squeeze bottle or paper cone with the flood icing in the center of the design. Apply light pressure and allow the icing to flow into the outline. The icing should not spread more than ½ in (1.3 cm) from the perimeter of the design. Stop and remove the cone. With a toothpick, move the icing to the outline. Work quickly, because the icing sets quickly.

4. Always work from the outside sections of a pattern toward the center. Never flood two adjoining sections at the same time. Flood widely separated sections and let the icing set before flooding the adjacent section. Flood icing sets in 15 to 20 minutes. When a flooded section is set, go back and fill in the empty sections next to it. Let the completed flooded sections dry overnight.

5. Carefully remove the masking tape or cut around the runout with an X-acto knife. Carefully remove the runout and peel back the plastic wrap. Attach the runout to an iced cake, plaque, or iced cookie using a metal spatula.

Lattice

Latticework in royal icing can be simple or complex. Lines of icing are piped with a round or star tip in one direction and then lines are piped across them to form a lattice pattern. This can be piped directly on a cake, plaque, or iced cookie.

1. Load 2 oz (57 g) of royal icing into a paper cone fitted with either a #2, #3, #4, or #5 round tip.

2. Position the tip at a 45° angle on the cake. Pipe a series of straight lines about ⅛ in (3 mm) apart. Pipe each line by applying a burst of pressure and raising the tip above the surface. Let the icing drop to the surface. Continue until all of the lines are piped in one direction.

3. Turn the cake until the crossover lines run toward your body. Go to the tip of the second line and extend the piping to the first line. Go to the tip of the third line and connect it to the first line. Continue this pattern until you reach the last line, which becomes the common line. Alternatively, turn the pattern half-turn and repeat the directions.

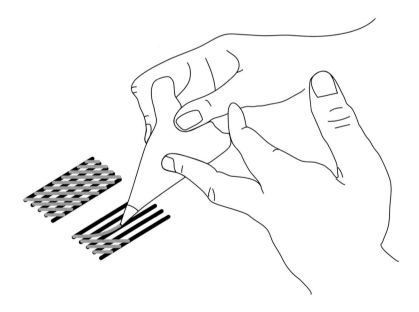

First, pipe lines all in the same direction, then pipe crossover lines, using the first line as the common line.

Swiss dots can be piped randomly or in a pattern to decorate a cake.

Swiss dots

This is perhaps the easiest of all the embroidery piping styles. Dots are piped all over the cake, either randomly or in an organized pattern. The key to Swiss dots is to soften the royal icing with a little water or pasteurized egg whites to the consistency of yogurt. No tip is used; instead, a tiny hole is snipped at the end of a small paper cone. When a dot is piped on the cake and the cone is pulled away, the tip of the dot rolls back to a round ball, leaving no head.

1. Load a small paper cone with 1 Tbsp (14 g) of flood icing, which is Meringue Powder Royal Icing softened with water or egg whites to the consistency of sour cream. Divide the surface of the cake into sections.

2. Snip the end of the paper cone with a pair of scissors and hold the tip at a 45° angle to the cake's surface or a 90° angle to the side of the cake. Apply light pressure and allow a small ball of icing to flow from the tip of the paper cone. Keep the tip stationary as you build up the ball of icing. Stop the pressure and remove the tip of the cone from the ball of icing. The icing will drop back and settle to make the surface of the ball completely smooth.

3. Randomly pipe balls of icing to form Swiss dots. Once you complete one section of the cake, pipe Swiss dots on the other sections.

Royal icing flowers

Royal icing flowers made from egg whites or meringue powder are a staple in the cake decorating industry. These hard-drying yet edible flowers can be piped weeks in advance on small pieces of parchment paper and then stored in containers with lids or in a small box. When ready to use them, the flowers are removed from the parchment paper with an offset metal spatula. The flowers are used to adorn formal cakes, cupcakes, and iced cookies. As a quick fix, they can dress up any cake. Attach them to an iced cake with a dab of royal icing, or place them directly on cupcakes iced in a soft icing. Royal icing flowers can also be petal-dusted for contrast.

BASIC FIVE-PETAL BLOSSOMS

Orange, apple, cherry, and peach blossoms, and forget-me-nots are all five-petal blossoms piped in exactly the same way. What makes each different is the color of the icing used: light pink for cherry blossoms, peach for peach blossoms, light orange for orange blossoms, natural white for apple blossoms, and sky blue for forget-me-nots.

1. Mix 1 oz (28 g) of Meringue Powder Royal Icing with the desired gel food color, or leave the icing white if making apple blossoms. Load the icing into a pastry bag fitted with a coupler. Attach a #101 or #102 tip to the pastry bag. Have a #6 or #7 icing nail and pieces of parchment paper handy.

2. Pipe a dot of icing on the icing nail. Put a parchment paper square on the dot. Hold the pastry bag in your writing hand and the icing nail in the other hand. Position the wide end of the piping tip in the center of the icing nail. Tilt your hands and the piping tip slightly to the right. With steady and even pressure, squeeze the pastry bag and drag the piping tip from the center of the nail, moving up about ½ in (1.3 cm) and pivoting to the right about ¼ in (6 mm). Then drag the piping tip back down to the point where you began. Both the starting and ending positions should come to a point. As you squeeze the pastry bag and move the piping tip, slowly rotate the icing nail counterclockwise.

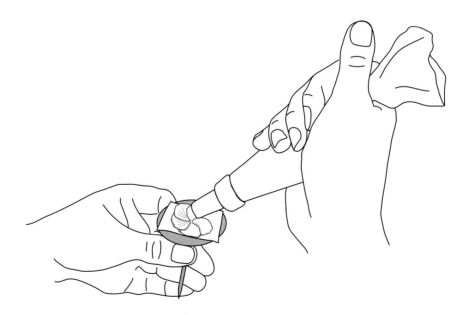

Rotate the icing nail as you pipe the icing and move the tip.

3. For the next petal, position the piping tip's wide end at the center point, next to the point of the first petal. Start slightly under the first petal. Repeat the procedure you used for the first petal, placing the petal next to the first. Repeat for the third and fourth petals. Overlap the fifth petal with the first, raising the tip slightly when moving back to the center point.

4. Mix 1 oz (28 g) of Meringue Powder Royal Icing with lemon yellow gel food color. Soften the icing with a few drops of water to prevent take-off points, and load 1 Tbsp (14 g) of the icing into a paper cone with a #2 round tip. Pipe five dots in the center of the flower to complete it.

Use this same technique to pipe all of these flowers, whether apple, orange, peach, or cherry blossoms, or forget-me-nots. If making forget-me-nots, the center can be dusted with a lemon yellow petal dust to finish.

VIOLETS

Violets are another type of five-petal blossom, in which not all the petals are the same size. The first two petals are the same size, and the last three are larger. The flower is completed with two yellow stamens pointing toward the two smaller petals.

1. Load a pastry bag with 4 oz (114 g) of deep violet royal icing. Attach a #101 or #102 petal-shaped tip to the bag. Load a small paper cone with a #2 round tip and ½ oz (14 g) of lemon yellow royal icing slightly softened with a few drops of water. Have an icing nail and pieces of parchment paper handy.

2. Pipe a dot of icing on the icing nail. Put a parchment paper square on the dot. Hold the pastry bag in your writing hand and the icing nail in the other hand. Position the wide end of the piping tip in the center of the icing nail. Tilt your hands and the piping tip slightly to the right. With steady and even pressure, squeeze the pastry bag and drag the piping tip from the center of the nail, moving up about ½ in (1.3 cm) and pivoting to the right about ¼ in (6 mm). Drag the piping tip back down to the center point where you began. Both the starting and ending positions should come to a point. As you squeeze the pastry bag and move the piping tip, slowly rotate the icing nail counterclockwise.

3. To pipe the second petal, position the piping tip's wide end at the center point, right next to the point of the first petal. Repeat the procedure you used for the first petal.

4. Skip a space on the icing nail by rotating the icing nail one petal-width. (Right-handed users turn the nail counterclockwise; left-handed users turn it clockwise.) The third, fourth, and fifth petals should be slightly separate from the first two as well as a little larger. Starting at the flower's center with the tip's wide end down, squeeze the pastry bag and move the tip upward about ¾ in (1.9 cm) and over about ¼ in (6 mm) and then drag the tip back to the flower's center, coming to a point. Repeat this for the fourth and fifth petals. Remember to ease up a little when bringing the fifth petal to the flower's center.

5. To finish the flower, pipe two points with yellow royal icing, starting at the center of the flower and dragging the points over the two smaller petals.

SWEET PEAS

Sweet peas are piped with one wide petal and two smaller petals in front of the larger petal. They come in a range of colors from subtle to bright, and can be two-toned as well. The petals are finished with a sepal and calyx.

1. Load a pastry bag with 4 oz (114 g) of royal icing in lavender, pink, or lemon yellow. Attach a #101 or #102 petal-shape tip to the bag. Load a small paper cone with ½ oz (14 g) of moss green royal icing and a #2 round tip. Have an icing nail and pieces of parchment paper handy.

2. Pipe a dot of icing on the icing nail. Put a parchment paper square on the dot. Hold the pastry bag in your writing hand and the icing nail in the other hand. Position the wide end of the piping tip in the center of the icing nail. Squeeze the pastry bag and turn the nail counterclockwise to form a large back petal.

3. Position the piping tip back at the flower's center. Pipe two smaller petals in front of the back petal, using the same technique as for the apple, cherry, peach, and orange blossoms on page 22.

4. For the sepals, position the #2 round tip with moss green icing at the left side of the flower. Pipe a small upward curve and end at the center. Do the same on the reverse side. Start at the bottom; squeeze the paper cone and pull in an upward curve. Stop the pressure and pull the tip toward you, leaving the center sepal suspended. For the calyx, position the tip at the bottom of the flower. Finish the flower by applying heavy pressure and then easing off as you pull a small tail.

Piped leaves

Leaves complete a floral spray by adding fullness and lushness. They can also be used alone as a decorating motif for a fall cake, and they are especially impressive when used with grapes and sweet pea clusters, or alone on cupcakes, or when added as a filler to piped rosettes or marzipan raspberries and blackberries. Several tips are used for leaf piping. The most common are the #67 (small leaf) tip and the #352 leaf tip. Both tips produce realistic-looking leaves; however, the #352 is the favorite of most decorators and designers because it pipes a quick and easy leaf without any fuss. The #67 tip requires extra-soft icing or royal icing, and the leaves tend to split unless your pressure control is precise. If using a #67 tip, Swiss Meringue Buttercream is usually soft enough to produce good results, but if your buttercream is too stiff, add ½ tsp (2.5 ml) of liquid to 4 oz (114 g) of buttercream for a softer consistency.

1. Fit a small paper cone with a #352 leaf tip. Add 1 Tbsp (14 g) of moss green buttercream or royal icing to the cone and carefully fold it closed.

2. Position the open side of this tip at a 45° angle. Apply a burst of pressure and leave the tip in place for a few seconds to build up the head of the shell, then pull the tip toward you. Stop the pressure. The leaf ends in a pointed tip, which is what you want. Leaves made with a #352 tip should be ¼ to ½ in (6 mm to 1.3 cm) long.

Leaves piped with a #67 or #68 leaf tip and a #352 leaf tip.

Piped rosettes

Rosettes are a staple in the world of cake decorating. They are typically piped from whipped ganache but can be made from buttercreams or whipped sweetened cream and royal icing.

1. Load a pastry bag with Meringue Powder Royal Icing and attach a #18 star tip. Position the bag at a 90° angle to the cake. If you are right-handed, start at the 9 o'clock position, and if left-handed, start at the 3 o'clock position. Raise the tip slightly from the surface. Pipe a tight circle without any space in the center. Once you pipe this one circle, stop the pressure but continue to move the tip in a continuous motion. Ease the tip away from the rosette.

2. To pipe a large rosette, you can use the same tip that you used for small rosettes but apply greater pressure, or you can use a #22 star tip or any giant star tip. Position the tip exactly as if you were piping a small rosette. When you pipe the first circle, leave a space in the center. Once you complete the circle, move the tip in a continuous circular motion inside the center of the rosette. Ease off the pressure and gently move the tip away from the rosette.

Gumpaste buds and blossoms

Gumpaste buds and blossoms are a decorator's best friend when used alone or in combination with gumpaste foliage (page 29). They quickly help decorate and beautify the most simplistic-looking cake. In fact, you can do a major floral spray of just blossoms, buds, and foliage for a breathtaking finish!

Blossoms

1. Measure out 1 oz (28 g) of gumpaste and color it with gel food colors, if desired. You can also leave the paste natural white and then petal-dust the dry flowers. Set aside a pea-size amount of paste. Cover the remainder with plastic wrap and place it in an airtight container.

2. Place the pea-size bit of gumpaste in your nonwriting hand. With the middle finger of your writing hand, rotate the paste into a round ball. Rotate one end of the ball to form a cone. Dip a modeling stick into a little cornstarch and then rotate the tip of the stick into the rounded edge of the cone. About ⅛ in (3 mm) of the stick should be in the cone.

3. Hold the modeling stick and cone at a 180° angle and place the X-acto knife at the base of the cone at a 45° angle. Cut five slits in the base of the cone, about ¼ in (6 mm) deep and equally spaced. Remove the paste from the modeling stick and open the slits. These are called florets. The bottom of the flower is called the trumpet.

4. Hold the trumpet part of the flower in your nonwriting hand. Position your thumb under one of the florets and your index finger on top, or vice versa. Pinch the floret with medium pressure to flatten the petal. Use your thumb to press around the petal to give it a more natural and rounded shape. Repeat the same technique until all of the florets are pressed into rounded petals. Press the tip of the modeling stick into the center of the flower to make a small cavity.

5. Make a small hook at one end of a 28-gauge florist wire. Dip the hook part into a little egg white, wiping off any excess. Thread the unhooked part into the cavity of the flower and pull the wire through the trumpet. When the hook reaches the cavity, rotate the trumpet until the hook is eased through the cavity. Apply light to medium pressure at the trumpet to secure the wire to the paste.

6. Stick the wired flower into the Styrofoam to allow the flower to dry. Drying time can be as little as 2 hours.

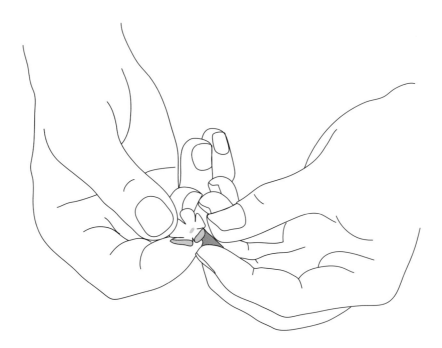

Pinch the floret to flatten the petal, then use your thumb to press around the petal for a more natural look.

Bud

1. To create a bud, rotate a pea-size amount of gumpaste into a round ball. Dip a wire (hooked or unhooked) in egg white and insert it inside the ball of paste. Secure the paste to the wire by pinching and pulling down on it.

2. Score five lines, equally spaced, around the top of the paste at a 45° angle. This flattens the paste by means of pressure. Rotate the center of the paste with your middle and index fingers until it looks like a bud. Place the bud on Styrofoam and let it dry. Drying time can be as little as 2 hours.

Petal-dusting

1. To finish the flower and bud, measure a tiny amount of pastel-colored petal dust, such as cosmos (pinkish) or lilac, as well as a small amount of moss green petal dust. If you choose a dark color, place a small amount of cornstarch in the center of your artist's tray. Use the cornstarch to dilute the color to a softer or lighter shade.

2. For the flower, brush a lighter shade of the color on each of the petals with the #3 sable paintbrush. Do not cover the entire petal with color; leave some of the paste's original color showing. This adds depth to the flower. Petal-dust each of the petals. Using a darker shade of the petal dust or a contrasting color, brush the tip of each petal. This adds contrast and shadows. Brush a little moss green petal dust inside the cavity of the flower and at the very bottom.

3. For the bud, brush the darkest tone of the petal dust underneath, extending it to the center of the bud. Brush moss green petal dust over the dark color to dilute it to a more natural tone. You can also add a touch of the dark petal dust to the center of the bud, which gives the illusion that the bud is flowering.

GUMPASTE FOLIAGE

A spray of gumpaste flowers or blossoms would not be complete without leaves and foliage. Leaves and foliage add dimension and fullness to a spray of flowers without overwhelming the spray. Leaves and spiral foliage can be used on their own, or in combination with gumpaste buds and blossoms, to add a simple elegance to any cake.

Cutter Leaves

1. Divide 2 oz (57 g) of gumpaste in half. Color each half a different shade of green (moss, leaf, forest, or mint). Wrap each half in plastic and place it in an airtight container.

2. Roll ½ oz (14 g) of green paste into a ball. Shape the ball into a log about 3 in (7.6 cm) long. Rub the work surface with solid vegetable shortening and place the log on it. With a nonstick rolling pin, press the center of the length of the log, rocking the pin back and forth to flatten the log. Roll the paste from the center to one side, preferably toward yourself. Roll it petal thin at one side of the center and gradually thicken it on the other side. The center should be no thicker than ⅛ in (3 mm).

3. Rub cornstarch on a clean area of the work surface. Place the flattened strip of gumpaste on the cornstarch. Cut out leaf shapes with rose, ivy, and hibiscus leaf cutters, positioning the cutters so the base of each leaf is on the thick part of the strip and the tip is on the thin part. Cut as many leaves as possible and place them under plastic wrap.

4. Repeat this technique with the rest of the green gumpaste.

Wiring and Adding Texture

1. To wire cut-out leaves, dip the tip of a 28-gauge florist wire into egg white and insert it into the thick part of the leaf about ¼ in (6 mm) deep. Wire all the leaves.

2. Place each leaf in a silicone leaf press and firmly press the top and bottom presses to give it texture. Soften each leaf by placing it on a cell pad and applying light to medium pressure with the dogbone tool around the edges. Dry the leaves on Styrofoam.

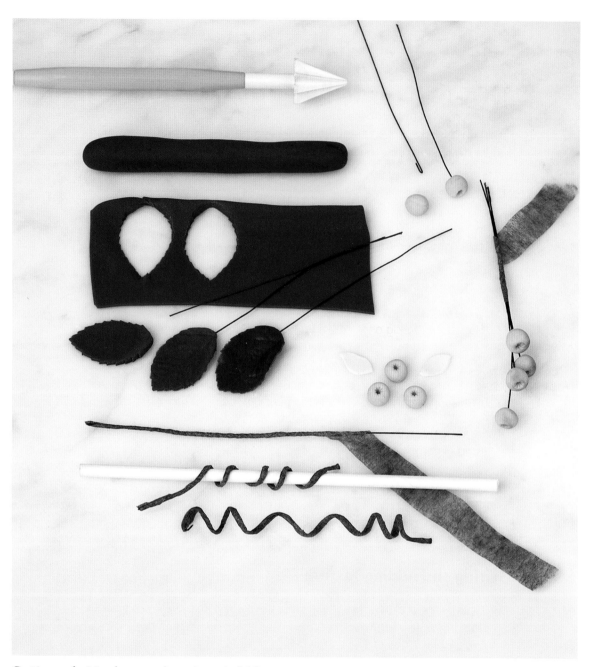

Cutting and wiring leaves and creating spiral foliage.

Petal-dusting

1. Adding petal dust to leaves helps bring them to life. Divide a small portion of green petal dust into three parts on an artist tray. Add a little cornstarch to one portion for a lighter tone, daffodil yellow to another portion for an autumn leaf, and leave the third portion as is. Have some burgundy or cosmos (pinkish) petal dust on your tray.

2. Brush the center of each leaf with the lighter green petal dust. Blend the color beyond the center of the leaf, but do not go near the edge. Turn the leaf over and do the same thing.

3. Brush the center of the leaf with the darkest green. This accents the veins and is used last at the very edge of the leaf. Turn the leaf over and do the same thing.

4. Add a little color—the green-yellow mixture or the cosmos—to the upper left corner of the leaf, where the sun would hit. Then brush the darkest green or burgundy color at the very edge. This gives the illusion that the sun has slightly scorched the edge of the leaf.

5. The color of each leaf can vary. Some leaves can be made deeper by using burgundy first and then adding dark green for the center and pink at the upper edge. Use real leaves as models or guides.

Creating a Shine

To give a natural shine to your leaves, pass them over a simmering kettle and allow the steam to coat them front and back. Pass each leaf several times to coat it. Allow the leaves to air-dry on Styrofoam.

Spiral Foliage

Take a long piece of 28-gauge green florist wire and tape it carefully with florist tape. Wrap the taped wire on a long dowel. Remove the taped wire to reveal the spiral foliage.

THE
CAKE DESIGNS

Anniversaries are a symbol of life-sharing. They show love, commitment, and prosperity. A cake decorated for an anniversary couple often looks much like a wedding cake. In fact, it can have the exact same components of a wedding cake. The cake can be several tiers tall or it can be a single large tier. The number of guests at the event would dictate the size of the tier(s). Often, an anniversary cake is not as elaborately decorated as most wedding cakes. It is more of an understatement and generally has a monogram, which includes the initials of the couple, but that isn't the case all of the time. In fact, for the anniversary cakes shown here, I have decided not to include monograms.

ANNIVERSARY CAKES

Brush Embroidery Cake

THE INSPIRATION

I WAS INSPIRED BY A BEAUTIFUL CAKE from a dear friend and colleague who lives in Western Australia. We were part of a group of international chefs from various parts of the world and we all assembled in Sao Paulo, Brazil. She brought with her a one-tier cake, iced in black rolled fondant and exquisitely painted with food colors. The result was one of the most beautiful cakes I have ever seen.

I wanted to do something similar with the same type of colors, but with a slightly different look and using a less intimidating technique than painting. So I chose brush embroidery in different colors to create my own take on this design, while still echoing the texture and color combination that had inspired me in the original cake.

THE CAKE

This is a one-tier cake, iced in black rolled fondant with brushed embroidered tulips, foliage, and a spray of gumpaste leaves and wild berries. This cake sits on an iced board and the brush embroidery extends to the cake board. This cake is suitable for almost any occasion but might work best as an anniversary cake. This could be an English-style Simnel cake with Almond-Vanilla Buttercream Icing, or a Devil's Food Cake with a Dark Chocolate Buttercream Icing. The cake is composed of two 10-in (25.4-cm) layers, iced and covered with fondant to a height of 4 in (10 cm).

THE TECHNIQUES

Brush Embroidery

1. Select a pattern (see Appendix, page 204) and trace the pattern onto see-through paper. Attach the pattern to the cake with masking tape or stick-pins. Transfer the pattern to the cake by pinpricking the pattern with a stickpin, making sure that the pin goes through the paper and punctures the cake to a depth of approximately 1/16 in (1.5 mm). The stickpin punctures should be close enough to get a good replica of the actual pattern. Once the transfer is complete, remove the paper to reveal the pattern likeness.

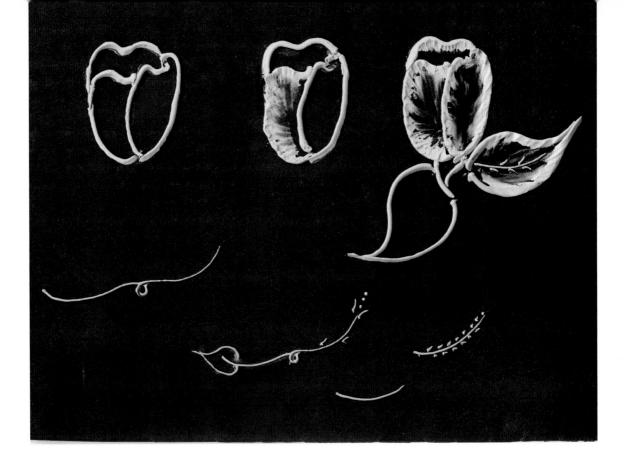

TOP ROW, FROM LEFT TO RIGHT: *A piped tulip and a tulip showing the stages of brush embroidery.*
BOTTOM ROW, FROM LEFT TO RIGHT: *Lines and curves forming freehand embroidery.*

2. Make a half-recipe of Meringue Powder Royal Icing and divide the icing among three bowls. Color one bowl with egg yellow food color, another bowl with a deep lilac food color, and a third bowl with moss green food color. Load three small paper cones with a #3 round metal tip and 1 oz (28 g) each of the three colored royal icings.

3. Review the Brush Embroidery technique on page 15. Begin outlining and brushing with the leaves, remembering to outline and brush one leaf at a time. Remember to dip the paintbrush in egg whites before doing the brushwork.

4. Next, outline and brush each of the petals, using the same technique as for leaves and remembering to outline and brush only one petal at a time.

5. Once the leaves and petals are brushed and dried, load a small paper cone with 1 Tbsp (14 g) of moss green icing and a PME #0 tip. Pipe veins in the leaves, remembering to start at the base of each leaf and drag the tip to the tip of the leaf. Go back and pull out stems from the center vein.

Gumpaste Leaves and Wild Berries

1. Make a half batch of Quick Gumpaste. Color 6 oz (170 g) a moss green color and 1 oz (28 g) a pale egg yellow.

2. For the leaves, measure out about 1 oz (28 g) of moss green gumpaste and roll it into a log about 8 in (23.3 cm) long onto a surface that has been lightly coated with shortening. Press a small rolling pin in the center to make an indentation and roll the paste from the center toward you (see Gumpaste Foliage on page 29). Using a large leaf cutter or rose cutter, cut out as many leaves as possible. Wire the leaves from the back with a

LEFT TO RIGHT: *A plain leaf, a petal-dusted gumpaste leaf, a wired berry, and a taped spray of berries.*

24-gauge florist wire, first dipped in egg whites. Press each leaf inside an all-purpose leaf veiner to give the leaves texture. Lightly soften the leaves on a cell pad with a dogbone tool. Let dry for 24 hours on a piece of Styrofoam. Make a total of 12 to 15 leaves.

3. Petal-dust with moss green color down the center of each leaf, and petal-dust the upper left-hand edge of each leaf with a deep lilac color. Steam the leaves over a simmering kettle for shine and let dry on Styrofoam for 24 hours.

4. For the wild berries, roll tiny balls of pale egg yellow gumpaste and wire with 28-gauge florist wire. Let dry on Styrofoam for 24 hours.

5. Steam the berries over a simmering kettle for shine. Let dry again on Styrofoam for another 12 to 24 hours.

6. When dry, wire bunches of blossoms into a spray and tape with florist tape.

7. To arrange, secure a walnut-size ball of gumpaste next to the cake with a dab of Meringue Powder Royal Icing. Let dry for 30 minutes. Cut the length of the wires on the wired leaves to approximately 1 in (2.5 cm) long, and cut the length of the wires on the blossom bunches to approximately 1 to 1½ in (2.5 to 3.8 cm) long, varying the lengths slightly to give some lightness and fullness to the arrangement. Arrange the leaves into the ball of gumpaste, then arrange the sprays of wild berries into the ball to complete the arrangement.

THE INSPIRATION

MY INITIAL INSPIRATION FOR THIS CAKE was something round and elegant with soft gumpaste flowers and beautiful embroidery piping. What changed my mind was an old movie I was watching that starred Marlene Dietrich in a tight-fitting hat with a scarf around it. That changed my motivation and I began to alter my design. I decided to alter the flowers for a bolder look, with some softness. The result is a fun piece with lots and lots of attitude!

THE CAKE

This is an 8-in (20.3-cm) sphere, iced in white rolled fondant. Freehand drapery, in two sections, is draped from the top of the sphere toward the bottom of the sphere and wrapped around the bottom of the cake. The cake is decorated with African Daisies and Chincherinchee, also known as Star of Bethlehem, as well as some freehand embroidery piping. The cake is made up of two half-spheres sandwiched with buttercream icing. The cake could be composed of a Silver White Cake with Italian Meringue Buttercream icing, or a Traditional Pound Cake iced with a Lime-Infused Buttercream Icing.

THE TECHNIQUES

Freehand Drapery

1. Roll out a piece of gumpaste into a 9 x 6-in (22.8 x 15.2-cm) rectangle. Fold both long ends in by ½ in (1.3 cm), creating a soft edge. Pleat the shorter ends in ½-in (1.3 cm) pleats. Pick up both ends and carefully pull and adjust the center of the drape for a more attractive fold. Attach one end to the top crown of the cake with a little water, drape slightly across and around the front of the cake, and extend the drape toward the back of the cake, attaching with a little water.

2. Create another drape of the same size and tuck the top end of the drape inside the previous drape to create a harmonious look. Attach to the cake with a little water. Continue to drape the second piece around the back of the cake and around the front of the cake, and tuck the bottom end inside the first drape for a complete look. For more information on Freehand Drapery, see page 11.

African Daisy

1. To make the base of the flower, take a grape-size piece of purple gumpaste and roll it into a round ball. Wire the ball with a piece of 24-gauge florist wire with a small hook at one end. Brush the ball with a little egg white and dip the ball into yellow cornmeal that has been colored with purple petal dust. Make sure the ball is completely coated and let dry on a piece of Styrofoam for 24 hours.

2. Once the base is dry, roll out about 25 tiny balls of purple gumpaste and three balls of yellow gumpaste. Attach the purple balls of paste to the base with egg whites. Dust with African violet petal dust. Then, add the yellow balls symmetrically on top of the base. Let dry for another 24 hours.

3. To make the petals, roll out a walnut-size piece of purple gumpaste into a log 6 to 8 in (15.2 to 20.3 cm) in length. Place a small rolling pin in the center of the log and apply pressure to make an indentation. From the center, roll the paste toward yourself as if you are making cut-out leaves (see page 29). Cut out petals with a small oval cutter, leaving one end petal thin and the other end about ⅛ to ¼ inch (3 to 6 mm) thick. The thick part is where the petal will be wired. Wire the petals with a 28-gauge florist wire. Roll out more paste and cut more petals to equal 16 petals. Dry the petals over a large rolling pin to achieve a natural curve to the petals. Let dry overnight.

4. When dry, dust each petal with African violet petal dust, starting at the top of the petal and fading the color toward the bottom. Set aside until ready to assemble.

5. To assemble, tape the petals under the base, two or three at a time and as close to the base as possible, with florist tape. Continue to tape petals to the base two or three at a time until you have all 16 petals around the base.

TOP ROW, LEFT TO RIGHT: *A grape-size piece of gumpaste for the center of the African Daisy and a wired, shaped petal.* BOTTOM ROW, LEFT TO RIGHT: *A semi-finished center with pea-size berries attached and a finished shaped petal.*

Chincherinchee (Star of Bethlehem)

1. For each blossom, take a pea-size amount of white gumpaste and shape it into a small ball, then shape it into cone shape, as if making a pulled blossom (see page 26). Cut 6 slits in each blossom. Pinch each petal with your thumb and index finger to a sharp point, then place the petal on a cell pad and shape each petal from the base of the flower to the tip with a dogbone tool, slightly cupping the petal.

2. Wire the blossom with a 28-gauge florist wire. Roll a minute piece of white gumpaste into a tiny ball. Place the ball inside the cavity of the flower with a little egg white. Continue to make and wire blossoms until you have a total of 6 flowers for each stem.

LEFT, TOP TO BOTTOM: *Shaping a pea-size bud into a blossom.* RIGHT, BOTTOM TO TOP: *A large cone-shaped center forms the base of the chincherinchee; the completed center; and a finished chincherinchee spray.*

3. For the buds, roll a tiny ball of white gumpaste into a rounded ball and attach to a piece of 28-gauge florist wire with a tiny amount of egg white. Slightly pinch the ball to a point. Let dry on Styrofoam. Continue to make and wire buds until you have a total of 6 buds for each stem.

4. For the stem, take a large pea-size piece of white gumpaste and shape it into a 1½-in (3.81-cm) cone. Wire with a 24-gauge florist wire. Let dry 1 hour.

5. When dry, turn the cone upside down and cut V shapes with a small pair of pointed scissors, starting near the wire. Alternate the positions of the cuts so that they lie between and above gaps in the previous rows. Slightly curve the tip of the cone and let dry on Styrofoam overnight.

6. The next day, petal-dust the cone with avocado green petal dust from the base of the cone to the middle, then add moss green petal from the middle to the tip of the cone.

7. To assemble, start taping the buds right up against the base of the cone. Evenly space the buds. Then, attach the blossoms, starting up against the buds. Tape firmly to complete the stem.

Australian
Stringwork Cake

THE INSPIRATION

I HAVE NEVER BEEN TO AUSTRALIA, but I have always been entranced with the elegant style of cake artistry this country brings to the industry. I have had several students in my New York–based classes who had never seen Australian stringwork, and it has been my pleasure to introduce them to the most beautiful style of cake décor there is; as least in my eyes. This cake was inspired by this unique style of cake artistry. Almost like a lacey skirt with strands of strings piped from the middle of the cake to the bottom bridge, Australian stringwork cakes still excite me whenever I get the chance to create one, and this cake, in a delicate shade of fuchsia, shows why.

THE CAKE

This is a 9-in (22.8-cm) rolled fondant round cake, which sits on a 12-in (30.4-cm) round board that is also iced in rolled fondant. The fondant is a pale fuchsia color. The cake has classic stringwork around the base, with drop strings on top of the stringwork as well as on the bottom of the bridge. Cornelli lace piping, lovely ribbons, and a beautiful floral spray add delicacy to the cake. This cake could be composed of Victoria Sponge Cake with an Almond-Vanilla Buttercream Icing, or Lemon Cream Pound Cake with Lemon-Infused Buttercream Icing.

THE TECHNIQUES

Australian Stringwork

MARKING THE CAKE

1. Wrap a strip of adding machine paper around the circumference of the Styrofoam cake. Measure the paper carefully so the ends meet around the cake but do not overlap. Fold the strip in half four times to create 16 equal sections.

2. Use the following chart to determine the width of the paper strip. Cut off any excess width.

Cake Height	Height of Strip
3-in- (7.6 cm) high cake	1¼ in (3.2 cm) high
4-in- (10.2 cm) high cake	1½ in (3.8 cm) high
5-in- (12.7 cm) high cake	1¾ in (4.4 cm) high

3. Position a round cookie cutter or a large glass at one end of the folded strip and draw a curve from one edge of the strip to the other. Carefully cut on the curved line. When the cut strip is unfolded, it will have a scalloped edge.

4. Attach the paper around the cake, about ¼ in (6 mm) above the bottom, with the scalloped edge down and the straight edge up. Secure the paper to the cake with masking tape or stickpins.

5. Score the top edge of the paper with a quilting wheel; this is where the extension work will begin. Then score the scalloped bottom of the paper; this is where the bridge work will begin. Remove the paper from the cake.

MAKING THE BRIDGE

1. Fill a small to medium-size paper cone with a #5 round metal tip and 1 Tbsp (14 g) of Egg White Royal Icing. Pipe a snail's trail (also called a bead or oval border) around the bottom of the cake with the #5 round tip.

2. For the bridge work, fill a small to medium-size paper cone with a #3 round metal tip and 1 Tbsp (14 g) of Egg White Royal Icing. Pipe the first row of the scalloped bridge following the mark made by the quilting wheel. Once you have gone completely around the cake, pipe the next row above and parallel to the first. Build the piped lines upward 5 to 7 times (see the progression of the bridge in the photo on page 54).

3. To smooth the bridge, brush 1 oz (28 g) of flood icing over it with a #3 sable paintbrush to cover any cracks and spaces between the piped lines. Let dry for 1 hour or overnight.

EXTENSION WORK

1. Rebeat 1 oz (28 g) of royal icing by hand in a small metal bowl, or use an offset metal spatula to smash the icing against a flat surface to get rid of lumps. Cut a small paper cone, fit it with a PME #0 tip, and load the re-beaten icing.

2. Starting at the top of the scored line, position the tip and touch the cake. Apply a burst of pressure at the start, creating a very small dot, then squeeze and pull the tip upward. Hold the string for a brief moment to dry slightly. Then bring the tip to the bottom of the bridge and break off the icing, or move the tip slightly under the bridge to break off. It is important to predict the length of the string by measuring the distance from the top of the line to the bottom of the bridge. This will take a few tries to get used to. Avoid pulling the stringwork directly down to the bridge as this will cause it to break often.

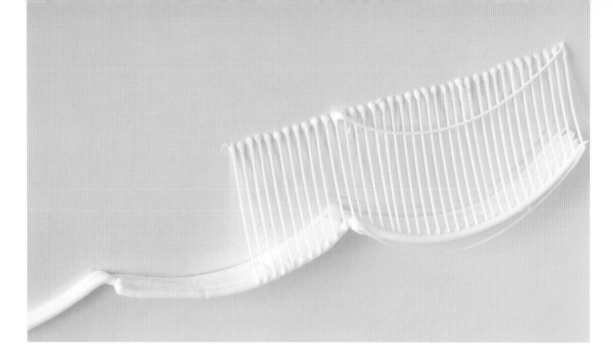

LEFT TO RIGHT: *Building the bridge, the extension work of the strings, and drop strings over the stringwork and below the bottom of the bridge.*

3. The strings should be spaced ⅟₁₆ to ⅛ in (1 to 3 mm) apart. Continue until you have completed the stringwork.

FINISHING THE STRINGWORK

1. Once the stringwork is complete, rebeat ½ oz (14 g) or Egg White Royal Icing and place it in a small paper cone with the #3 round tip (the same tip used in the building of the bridge).

2. Pipe a finishing line on the bridge to give a tailored-look to the bridge-work. Thus, if you initially piped 5 lines to build up the bridge, then this would be the sixth and final line.

TRELLIS OR DROP-STRING PIPING

1. Rebeat ½ oz (14 g) of Egg White Royal Icing and place it in a small paper cone with the same #3 round tip just used to pipe a finishing line on the bridge.

2. Pipe drop strings on top of the stringwork at each scallop by applying a burst of pressure, pulling the sting about 1½ in (3.8 cm) long, and allowing the string to drape over a scalloped section and end at the top of the next section. The drop string should extend less than half the distance of the vertical piped stringwork.

3. Pipe another row of drop strings at the bottom of the bridge. The drop strings here should be just a hair off the surface of the cake board. Finish the top of the bridge with fabric ribbons and cornelli-lace piping above the ribbons. These additional features will add elegance and style to the cake.

Floral Spray

The floral spray is a simple spray of five-petal pulled blossoms with buds and gumpaste leaves. All the techniques needed to create this floral spray are on pages 22–31. Small, light-colored ribbon twists and beautiful large deep fuchsia ribbons give this cake the finishing touch it needs.

Birthday cakes are a tradition that goes back centuries. The annual celebration of the day of one's birth is a ritual that continues to this day, and often, a special cake is presented to the birthday person. In the late-Victorian era, birthday cakes were elaborate, almost as elaborate as wedding cakes. These were usually single-tier cakes. Today, birthday cakes in the United States are very simple and often have a greeting on top of the cake. In other countries, greetings may or may not be added. The birthday cakes shown here are unusual as they are quite elaborate and unique cakes, and none include a birthday greeting.

BIRTHDAY CAKES

THE INSPIRATION

MY INSPIRATION FOR THIS CAKE is a neighbor I knew decades ago. She was a church-going lady with exquisite hats. Whenever Ms. Constance "stepped out," she was "decked out." Always impeccably dressed, she took pride in her appearance and her hats were her prize-winning accessory. This hat design is my dedication to her and the joy she brought to me and many others.

THE CAKE

This is a 10-in (25.4 cm) half-sphere or dome-shaped cake, covered in egg yellow rolled fondant. The cake size is extended with a large rim about 16 in (40.6 cm) in diameter, textured with a textured rolling pin. The cake is decorated with two-toned ribbons and dark foliage and a stunning large gardenia. This dome-shaped cake could be composed of Victorian Sponge Cake, filled with a frozen raspberry puree and iced with Lemon-Infused Buttercream Icing, or Cream Cheese Pound Cake iced with French Vanilla Buttercream.

THE TECHNIQUES

Gardenia

1. Make the calyx by rolling out a tiny amount of olive green gumpaste on a little white vegetable shortening. Cut one large calyx with a rose calyx cutter. Place the calyx on a dry surface.

2. For the petals, measure out 2 oz (57 g) of white gumpaste. Color ½ oz (14 g) of the white paste a dark olive green. Wrap in plastic wrap and set aside. Take the balance of the white paste and roll out thinly on a tiny amount of white vegetable shortening. Cut out 6 large petals with a rose petal cutter. Flute or soften each petal with a dogbone tool on a cell pad.

3. Brush the green calyx with a tiny amount of egg white and arrange the petals symmetrically on the green calyx—placing the base of the petals directly onto the calyx. The petals will slightly overlap. Place tiny amounts of cotton under the petals to maintain the shape of the petals as they dry.

CREATING A GARDENIA, CLOCKWISE FROM BOTTOM RIGHT: *Two overlapped white petals on a green calyx, an almost-completed gardenia with cotton between the layers, and the final five twisted petals that will complete the flower.*

4. Roll out additional white gumpaste and cut out 6 medium-size petals. Soften the edges of the petals. Brush egg white at the center point of the 6 large petals and arrange the 6 medium-size petals on top of the large petals. Prop up the petals with tiny amounts of cotton.

5. Roll out the balance of the white gumpaste and cut out eight small petals. Soften all 8 of the petals. Arrange 3 of the 8 petals on top of the medium-size petals and prop up with cotton. Then take the last 5 petals and arrange them in a fan shape, overlapping each other slightly. Twist the petals near the bottom. Cut off approximately ½ in (1.3 cm) of the twisted paste from the bottom and place the fan-shaped petals directly on top of the 3 other small petals with a tiny amount of egg white. Prop up with cotton and allow to dry on Styrofoam for 24 hours.

6. For the leaves, roll out the olive green gumpaste and cut out 5 large leaves, using the techniques for Gumpaste Foliage on page 29. Emboss the leaves with an all-purpose leaf veiner and slightly soften the edges of the leaves. Allow to dry on Styrofoam and then pass the leaves over a steam kettle to add shine. Allow to dry overnight.

Two-Toned Ribbons

1. Roll out 2 oz (57 g) of moss green gumpaste and 2 oz (57 g) of egg or canary yellow gumpaste on a work surface rubbed with a tiny amount of white vegetable shortening. The paste should be ⅛ in (3 mm) thick. Sandwich one strip on top of the other and reroll the paste until it is between 1⁄16 and ⅛ in (1.5 mm and 3 mm) thick. Cut out strips about 1 in (2.5 cm) wide and 5 in (12.7 cm) long. Score the very edge of each strip with a quilting wheel.

2. Shape a 24-gauge florist wire into a U. Insert the U into the gumpaste strip to a depth of about ¼ in (6 mm). Brush a little egg white over the wire to secure it and then bend the strip over into a closed U shape.

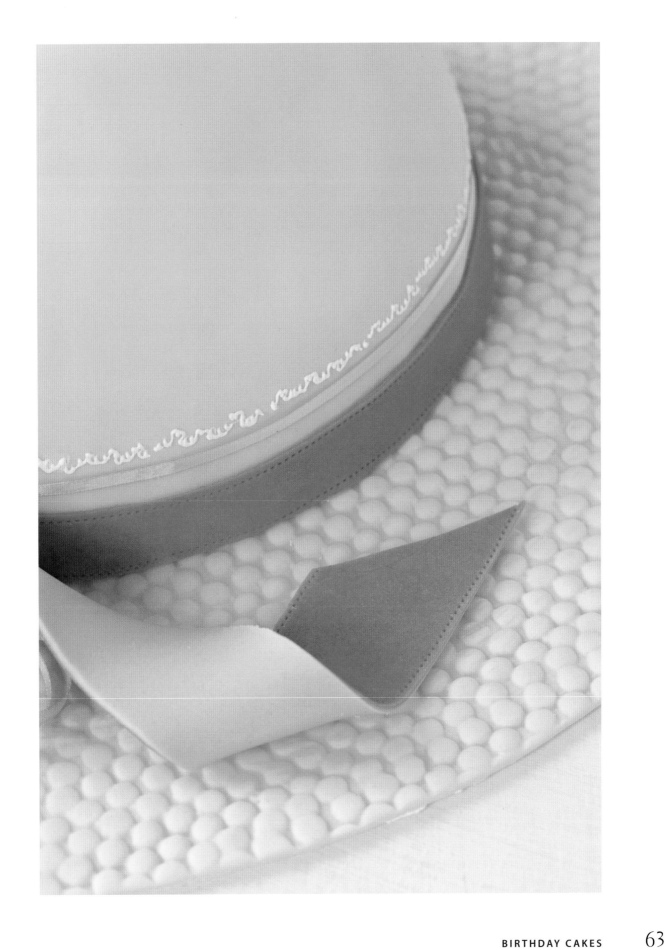

Large Leaves

1. Color 2 oz (57 g) of gumpaste a dark leaf green or olive green and wrap in plastic wrap. Remove ¼ oz (7 g) green paste and shape it into a rounded ball. Rub a tiny amount of white vegetable shortening on the work surface. Place the ball on the work surface and use a nonstick rolling pin to roll it into a log about 3 in (7.6 cm) long.

2. Brush a little egg white on a 24-gauge green or white florist wire and insert the wire into the log of gumpaste to a depth of about ½ in (1.3 cm). Pinch the end of the paste to secure it to the wire.

3. Rub a tiny amount of white vegetable shortening on the work surface and place the wired gumpaste on it. Press a nonstick rolling pin in the center of the paste to flatten it slightly. Thin the left and right sides of the paste with a modeling stick, leaving a ridge in the center. Part of the center ridge contains the inserted wire. With a modeling stick, thin the ridge above the inserted wire.

4. Place the wired paste on the work surface with the end of the wire at the 12 o'clock position. Position an X-acto knife at the end of the paste to the left of the wire at a 45° angle. Drag the knife across the paste, making an oval shape from the back to the front. Stop the curve at the 6 o'clock position. Reposition the knife at a 45° angle at the end of the paste to the right of the wire. Drag the knife, making a curve that meets the left curve at the center point of the leaf. Remove the excess paste and lift the leaf from the wire.

5. Place the leaf on an all-purpose leaf press. Emboss the leaf. Slightly soften the edges of the leaf with a dogbone tool. Let dry for several hours or overnight.

6. When completely dry, pass the leaf blades over steam from a simmering kettle to create condensation. This gives a natural shiny look to the leaves. Let dry overnight. The large leaf is complete.

Texture on Hat Brim

1. Roll out 16 oz (454 g) of canary yellow or egg yellow rolled fondant. Roll the paste onto a small amount of cornstarch, about ¼ in (6 mm) thick and about 16 in (40.6 cm) in diameter.

2. Roll a textured rolling pin (a bubble-wrap rolling pin) on top of the paste until it is a thickness of about ⅛ in (3 mm). Cut out a 16-in (40.6-cm) round circle with a pizza wheel.

3. Brush a 16-in (40.6-cm) round cake drum with a tiny amount of water and place the textured paste onto the drum. Place a small amount of royal icing onto the center of the textured paste and place the half-sphere, fondant-iced cake in the center.

A textured rolling pin is rolled over yellow-green rolled fondant to reveal the texture used on the hat brim.

Nirvana Cake

THE INSPIRATION

MY INSPIRATION FOR THIS CAKE was formed when I was in Lisbon, Portugal. The beautiful colored homes in pastel shades of pinks, lavender, blues, and whites gave me the idea of using these colors together in a Nirvana cake. Nirvana is an old English- and South African–style cake decorating technique. The cake, usually a fruitcake, is iced in marzipan and then re-iced several times in royal icing. The cake is decorated with large runouts or flooded panels around the sides with see-through openings, and large flooded panels on the top and bottom of the cake. The cake is decorated with overpiped lines, which give a lot of dimension to the cake, and with additional flooded panels on top of the base panels, which give the illusion of a larger and more elaborate cake. The result is a cake that looks more like a music box or an enclosed carousel.

THE CAKE

This is an 8 x 6-in (20.3 x 15.2-cm) cake. The cake is iced and decorated in multiple shades of lavender royal icing with lots and lots of details. This is a Simnel cake (an English-style cake), and this rendition is a delightful twist on a very light fruitcake that is loaded with flavor and almond paste. In the English tradition, the cake would be iced in marzipan and then with several coats of royal icing. In the United States, we would typically skip the marzipan and royal icing and ice the cake with Almond-Vanilla Buttercream Icing or Italian Meringue Buttercream and then cover the cake with rolled fondant. But for the sake of authenticity, I have iced the cake shown here in the traditional English style of royal icing.

THE TECHNIQUES

Side Panels

1. Select the patterns for the Nirvana cake (see Appendix, pages 205–208). The side panel pattern is a rectangular shape with a diamond-shaped center cutout. Make 8 photocopies of the pattern, tape each one onto a large cardboard, and cover with plastic wrap. This cake has 6 rectangular side panels, but it would be wise to make 8, in case of breakage.

2. Outline the panels with a #3 round tip and Egg White Royal Icing.

3. To make flood/runout icing from Egg White or Meringue Powder Royal Icing, use pasteurized egg white to soften the royal icing to flood or runout consistency. Flood the panels (see the Flooding/Runouts technique on page 17) and let for dry 24 to 48 hours. Set the panels aside.

Top and Bottom Panels

1. Copy the pattern for the top, bottom and top overlay (see Appendix, page 206). Note that all three are labeled on the same pattern, so it is important to pay attention to the arrows specifically for the pattern you are working on.

2. For Bottom Panel A, you can either outline and flood the panel on a plastic wrap–covered cardboard, let it dry for 48 hours, and then carefully attach it to the iced cake board with royal icing; or you could transfer the drawing directly to the iced cake board and then outline and flood the panel directly onto the iced board. The latter is the safest way to do this style of work.

3. For Bottom panel B, make 6 copies of this pattern (see Appendix, page 205) and tape onto a cardboard and cover with plastic wrap. Outline all 6 panels and flood in a contrasting color or a lighter or deeper shade of icing than that used for Bottom Panel A. Let dry for 24 hours.

4. Bottom Overlay. This is a separate panel that actually hides the negative spacing when the side panels are assembled next to the edge of Bottom Panel A. Make 6 copies of the pattern (see Appendix, page 205), tape onto a cardboard, and cover with plastic wrap. Outline all 6 panels and flood in the same color as the side panels. Let dry for 24 hours.

5. Top Panel A is a large panel with a donut hole in the center. Make 1 copy of this pattern (see Appendix, page 206) and tape onto a cardboard and cover with plastic wrap. Outline and flood the panel, using the same color as for Bottom Panel A. Let dry for 48 hours. Set aside.

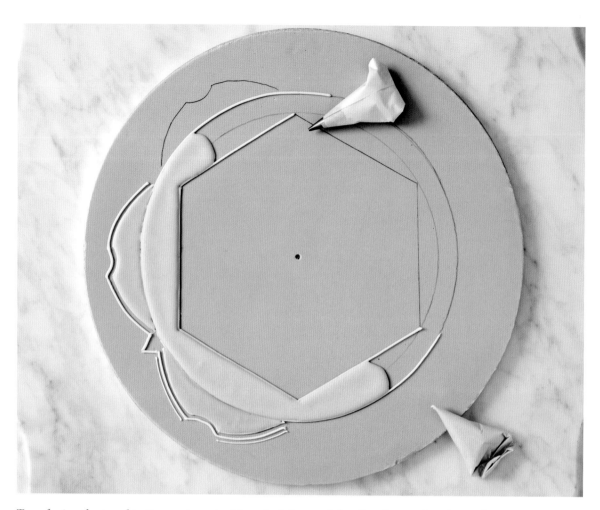

Transferring the panel pattern onto an iced board, piping, and flooding Bottom Panel A and Bottom Panel B.

6. Top Overlay A. Make 6 copies of this pattern (see Appendix, page 205) and tape onto a cardboard and cover with plastic wrap. Outline and flood all 6 panels using the same color as for Bottom Panel B. Let dry for 24 hours. These panels will be placed near the edge of Top Panel A.

7. Top Overlay B sits on top of Top Panel A and actually encloses the cake from the top view. Make 1 copy of Top Overlay B (see Appendix, page 206) and tape onto a cardboard and cover with plastic wrap. Outline and flood the panel using a different shade of lavender than that used for Top Panel A, or the same shade as used for the Side Panels. Let dry for 48 hours.

Ovals and Monogram

1. Copy the oval pattern (see Appendix, page 207) and tape onto a cardboard and cover with plastic wrap. Outline and flood 6 ovals a shade of lavender different from that used for the side panels. Let dry for 12 hours. Set aside.

2. Copy the monogram pattern (see Appendix, page 208) and tape onto a cardboard and cover with plastic wrap. Outline and flood the monogram using the same shade as for the ovals. Let the monogram dry for 24 hours before removing. The monogram will sit directly on top of the cake.

Plunger Flowers

1. Make up to 3 dozen small plunger flowers using the technique described on page 10.

To Assemble

1. Place the iced cake in the middle of the cake board and inside Bottom Panel A. Secure the cake with a small amount of Meringue Powder Royal Icing.

2. Attach Bottom Panel B to the edge of Bottom Panel A. Secure each panel with a small amount of Meringue Powder Royal Icing.

3. Attach the side panels around the sides of the cake. Pipe a small amount of Meringue Powder Royal Icing at the bottom of one side panel and on the side of the panel that will face in toward the cake, and place the panel inside Bottom Panel A. Place an object next to the panel to prevent it from falling and breaking. Attach the next panel, making sure that the panel is glued to the previous panel with Meringue Powder Royal Icing. Place a small object next to this panel to prevent it from falling. Add additional side panels, using small objects to hold the panels in place until all six side panels have been added around the cake. Fill in any negative spacing on the side panels with Meringue Powder Royal Icing. Let dry for 30 minutes to secure the panels.

    Note: When attaching the side panels, many of the panels won't fit snugly inside Bottom Panel A. Care should be taken as these panels are made of royal icing and not gumpaste and are thus not flexible. This is where the Bottom Overlay will be used to make a more attractive fit.

4. Place the Bottom Overlay panels next to the side panels to cover any negative spacing. Attach these panels with Meringue Powder Royal Icing.

5. Attach plunger flowers to the flooded ovals with a tiny amount of Meringue Powder Royal Icing. To create tiny leaves, roll out a small amount of gumpaste very thinly on a tiny amount of vegetable shortening, then place the rolled-out gumpaste on a surface lightly dusted with cornstarch. Use a medium-size rose calyx cutter to cut out a calyx, then cut off each of the 5 sepals from the calyx to form 5 tiny leaves. Use dots of royal icing to attach the leaves to the ovals, flanking the plunger flowers.

6. Attach the ovals to the cake, inside the side panel cutouts, with royal icing.

7. Load a small paper cone with a #3 round tip and ½ oz (14 g) of Meringue Powder Royal Icing. Pipe a line of icing on top of each of the side panels. This will hold Top Panel A to the side panels. Carefully remove the plastic wrap from Top Panel A and carefully place this on top of the side panels.

8. Carefully remove the monogram from the plastic wrap. Carefully place the monogram on top of Top Overlay B, adding a tiny amount of Meringue Powder Royal Icing under the monogram to secure it to Top Overlay B.

9. Load a small paper cone with a #3 round tip and ½ oz (14 g) of Meringue Powder Royal Icing. Pipe a line of icing on the inside edge of Top Panel A. This line of icing will act as a glue for Top Overlay B. Carefully place Top Overlay B on top of Top Panel A. Carefully remove Top Overlay A panels and attach to Top Panel A, mirror-imaging the Bottom Overlays.

10. For a raised look to the cake and the monogram on top, load a small paper cone with a #3 round tip and ½ oz (14 g) of Meringue Powder Royal Icing. Position tip about ¼ in (6 mm) from the outside edge of the Bottom Overlays. Pipe a line outlining the panels. Continue until all of the panels have been shadow-piped. Connect the ends of each shadow-piped line and end it in a V shape. Repeat this for all of the Bottom Overlay panels. Use the same technique for the monogram on top of Top Overlay B (see finished cake).

Bottom Panel A is partially flooded and attached to a large iced board, and Bottom Panel B is attached to Bottom Panel A. The side panels are attached inside Bottom Panel A, flooded ovals are attached through the side panels, and Bottom Overlay A is attached to the bottom of the side panel for a more attractive finish.

Tiffany-Inspired
Ribbon Cake

THE INSPIRATION

SOMETHING SMALL, SOMETHING PRETTY, AND SOMETHING BLUE—these concepts were the inspiration for this precious piece. I love Tiffany works, and of course a Tiffany box is a lovely gift all in itself. But here, I wanted to create a cake that was loosely inspired by Tiffany, but not exactly a replica of the Tiffany box shape or colors. Shades of blues and light fuchsia were my focus for this cake.

THE CAKE

This is a small rectangular cake in shades of blues. There are large gumpaste ribbons in a darker blue, with pale pink gumpaste ribbons on top of the blue. This is finished off with a vertical-style bow with streamers and a cameo mold with plunger flowers in the center. On top is a soft painting of a pansy spray that is muted with a pearl luster spray and some embroidery piping around the spray. Here a Banana-Rum Cake with a Coconut-Rum Buttercream Icing would be my immediate choice.

THE TECHNIQUES

Pansy Spray Painting

1. Select the Pansy Spray pattern (see Appendix, page 208). Trace and transfer the pattern directly to the surface of the cake, using a stickpin to transfer, or to a small sugar plaque, using the carbon transfer method (see page 15). Gather an artist tray and the colors you will need for the spray. The pansy itself can be a lemon or egg yellow, violet, purple, lavender, pinkish, or dusty rose. Include foliage colors, such as mint, leaf, or forest green. Shadow colors and highlight colors will complete the painting. The shadow color can be a chocolate brown, violet, black, or a deeper shade of any pastel color. For highlights, use full-strength liquid whitener. Add liquid whitener to gel food colors to achieve a pastel tone.

2. Select the gel color for the pansy petals and squeeze a dot of the gel into the artist tray or onto a small plastic plate. Squeeze a dot of liquid whitener next to the chosen color. Mix the two to achieve a pastel tone. Squeeze the green color for the leaves and a dot of liquid whitener next to the green. Mix a small portion of the green and white together and leave the rest unmixed. This will be the leaf color and the shadow color for the leaves.

3. For the highlighter, squeeze another dot of liquid whitener on another section of the tray along with a dot of the shadow color or the color to be used for the pansy. Three sable paintbrushes—fine, small, and medium— should also be nearby on the workstation. Prepare two small containers of water for cleaning the brushes and diluting food colors as needed.

4. Start with the leaves by dipping the fine brush into water and then into the shadow green color. Trace the pattern outline with the green color. Dip the brush in water to clean it and then outline the pansy with the appropriate shadow color.

5. With the small sable paintbrush, paint a deeper edge of the shadow green color inside the leaves. Using a little water, brush the edge of the green to fade the color toward the center of the leaf. Paint a thicker border around the pansy with the shadow color, using the same technique as for the leaves. Brush the deeper color of the pansy with a little water to thin the edge of the shadow color.

6. Go back to the leaves. Thin a little of the mixed green color (green with liquid whitener) with water and begin to fade this color inside the leaf with the medium brush. Use very little water, which can dilute the color too much or make the painting too wet. Do this to all of the leaves.

TOP: *The stages of painting a pansy spray with gel food colors.* BOTTOM: *The completed painted pansy spray.*

7. For the pansy, begin to fade in the mixed color (chosen color and liquid whitener), using a little water with the medium brush. Use long strokes as you brush the color toward the center of the flower.

8. Go back to the leaves and paint in the veins with a deeper color or the shadow color for the pansy. Return to the pansy and fade in the highlight. Let the painting dry for 2 hours before adding the center to the pansy.

9. Using the fine brush, paint a circle in the middle of the pansy with a highlight color or a different bright color. With a deeper color, paint tiny stamens around the circle with the fine brush.

10. Spray the painting with a thin coating of edible pearl spray. The painting is complete.

Embroidery Piping

See the embroidery piping techniques on page 9. Finish off the top of the cake with some embroidery piping around the painting.

Ribbons

1. Measure the circumference of the cake and cut a strip of adding machine paper or parchment paper to serve as a guide for the length of the ribbon.

2. Measure out 8 oz (20.3 g) of gumpaste. Separate 4 oz (114 g) and color it a bluish-green color. This will be the bottom ribbon strip. The balance should remain white. This will be the top ribbon strip.

3. Roll out the paste to about ⅛ in (3 mm) thick on a work surface lightly coated with shortening. Cut each ribbon to the length of the paper guide, using an X-acto knife. The bottom ribbon should be approximately 2½ in (6.35 cm) wide and the top ribbon should be approximately 1¼ in (3.18 cm) wide. Stitch the edges of both ribbons with a quilting wheel.

4. To assemble, brush the center area of the bottom ribbon with a pastry brush and a tiny amount of water. Carefully place the top ribbon on top. Attach to the cake with a tiny amount of water.

Large Bow and Cameo

1. Roll and cut out 4 additional ribbon strips—2 white and 2 blue—for the bow and streamers, using the same technique as for the ribbons, and let dry. Brush 1 blue strip with a tiny amount of water with a pastry brush, from one end to the other. Attach a white strip on top of the blue strip. Do the same for the other white and blue strips.

2. For the large bow, brush a little water in the center of 1 ribbon strip. Raise one end and attach it to the center of the bow strip. Attach the second end to the center of the bow strip. Place cotton between the loops of the bow and allow it to dry for several hours.

3. For the streamers, cut the other blue and white strip in half, making 2 strips. With an X-acto knife, cut a V shape at one end of the strip, about ½ in (1.3 cm) deep. Cut another V shape at one end of the other strip about ½ in (1.3 cm) deep.

4. Take ½ oz (14 g) of white gumpaste and knead it well. Place the gumpaste into a cameo mold and press firmly. Release the cameo and let dry for 15 minutes. Trim the edge of the cameo with an X-acto knife and let the cameo dry for several hours.

5. Attach the cameo to the center of the bow with a small amount of Meringue Powder Royal Icing. Decorate around the cameo with plunger flowers (see page 10 for instructions on making plunger flowers).

Groom's cakes have always been considered a Southern tradition in the United States. Often the groom's cake is a chocolate cake or a cheesecake, and in the distant past, a fruitcake. It is generally placed on a separate table from the bridal table and usually served to the head table—the table of the bride, groom, and their family or wedding party. Sometimes, it is cut and served and given away as a wedding favor. Groom's cakes come in many different shapes, sizes, and colors, and often reflect a theme that relates to the groom's hobbies or interests in some way.

GROOM'S CAKES

Venetian Mask Cake

THE INSPIRATION

VENICE WAS MY INSPIRATION for this artistic piece. As I walked the streets of Venice with my good friend and colleague Gian Paolo and his lovely family, I wanted to buy everything in sight, but what were most impressive were the masks. The array of masks was endless, from stunningly beautiful to almost grotesque, and from the simplest to the most ornate, with tons of feathers, ribbons, and vibrant colors. I chose to do something on the simpler side for this cake, as I wanted this mask to be more masculine and fitting for a groom's cake.

THE CAKE

I chose a triangle-shaped cake to depict a more masculine image, iced with lots and lots of chocolate rolled fondant with gold and chocolate ribbons around the bottom edge of the cake. The cake features two dramatic drapes—one in front and one, which is not visible in the photo shown here, in back. The cake is placed at an angle in the center of a large square board that is also covered with chocolate rolled fondant. On top sits a dramatic Venetian mask, sprayed in chocolate and gilded and sprayed with a high gloss.

The cake, of course, is chocolate. The Devil's Food Cake with Dark Chocolate Buttercream Icing is the perfect choice for this confection. However, for those who don't prefer chocolate, the Cream Cheese Pound Cake with French Vanilla Buttercream could be a close second.

THE TECHNIQUES

The Mask

1. Select the pattern for the Venetian Mask (see Appendix, page 209). Trace the mask onto parchment paper. Roll out 8 oz (228 g) of gumpaste about ⅛ in (3 mm) thick on a tiny amount of vegetable shortening. Place the pattern onto the mask and carefully cut out the mask with an X-acto knife. Let the cutout rest for 15 minutes on a surface that has been dusted lightly with cornstarch.

TOP: *A paper mask template.* BOTTOM: *A gumpaste cutout of the mask.*

2. If you have an appropriately shaped plastic or porcelain mold, dust the interior of the mold with a light coating of cornstarch, carefully place the gumpaste mask into the mold, and let rest for 30 minutes. Remove the gumpaste mask after 30 minutes to check to see if it is sticking to the mold. Re-dust the mold, if necessary, and place the gumpaste mask back into the mold. Let rest for several hours, checking from time to time to see if it is sticking. Let rest in the mold for 48 hours. Remove the gumpaste mask from the mold, and let it rest for an additional 48 hours to allow it to dry on the inside. When dried, carefully sand with fine sandpaper.

3. If you do not have a plastic mold, after cutting the gumpaste mask out using the pattern, let the cutout dry for 5 minutes on a surface that has been lightly dusted with cornstarch. Place a tiny piece of cotton under the "nose" of the mask. Place your thumb and index finger into the eye socket of the cut-out mask and gently squeeze together to help give a protruding shape to the nose. Take your thumb and index finger and gently stroke the left and right sides of the nose. This will give the nose more definition. Let dry for 1 to 2 hours. Pick up the gumpaste mask and see if it will stand on its own when you slightly bend back both sides of the mask. If the mask is still limp and doesn't stand on its own, then let it rest for another couple of hours. Once the cutout is firm enough, slightly bend both sides of the mask so that it will stand on its own. For the two ends of the mask, slightly stroke the mask from the front side, giving it a slight indentation at the sides (see photo). Let the mask dry for 48 hours and then lightly sand with fine sandpaper.

SPRAYING THE MASK

1. Melt equal parts dark chocolate and cocoa butter and mix them together. Load the chocolate mixture into the spray container of a Wagner Spray Gun or the cup that is attached to the sprayer of an airbrush. Test an area on newspaper until the chocolate mixture starts to coat.

2. Place the mask on a piece of newspaper and make sure that you have covered the entire area around the mask with newspaper as well. Position yourself about 1½ feet (46 cm) away from the mask and begin to spray it lightly, in layers. Turn the mask over and spray the inside. Let the mask dry for 48 hours. For a deeper color, re-spray the mask again after 48 hours and let dry for an additional 48 hours.

GILDING THE MASK

1. Mix gold powder with a tiny amount of alcohol. Using a #0 fine paint-brush, outline the edge of the mask with the gold powder, including the interior of the eyes.

2. Pipe a rope border around the eyes, using a #2 round tip and ½ ounce (14 g) of royal icing. Let dry for several hours and then gild over the rope. Paint 4 gilded curves in the middle of the mask (see photo).

LEFT: A fully formed, partially sprayed mask.
RIGHT: The mask fully sprayed in chocolate, decorated, and gilded.

Freehand Drapery

See page 11 for instructions on creating Freehand Drapery. Create two drapes and attach one to the top center of the cake, extending down the front of the triangle to the cake board, and the other down the back side of the cake.

Bamboo Cake

THE INSPIRATION

THE IDEA FOR THIS CAKE came from my visit to Lisbon, Portugal. My guide and driver, Zé, took me all over this lovely country with its multi-colored homes and castles, including a trip to their 1998 expo, where I saw the tallest bamboo plants I have ever seen. This cake was made in his honor.

THE CAKE

This is a small 6-in (15-cm) round cake, iced in mint green rolled fondant. Rectangular pieces of gumpaste are fitted around 1-in (2.5-cm) wooden dowels to form the bamboo cylinders, and strips of gumpaste made with a clay gun form the sections around the bamboo. The bamboo stalks are airbrushed in a variety of green colors. This is a Banana-Rum Cake with Lemon-Infused Buttercream Icing.

THE TECHNIQUES

Bamboo

1. First, you will need six 1 x 6-in (2.5 x 15-cm) round dowels. Sand the edges of the dowels with fine sandpaper for a smoother edge. Roll out a rectangular piece of gumpaste on a surface lightly rubbed with a tiny amount of vegetable shortening, and cut the paste to about 3½ x 6 in (9 x 15.2 cm). Cut out about a dozen more rectangular pieces of the same size, and let dry for 15 to 20 minutes.

2. Dust the dowels with a small amount of cornstarch. Place a wooden dowel inside one edge of one of the gumpaste rectangles, and roll up the paste to form a round cylinder. Cut any excess off with an X-acto knife or pizza wheel. The paste can overlap by ¼ in (6 mm). Glue the edge with a tiny amount of egg white, and press firmly but carefully. Repeat to make about 12 to 18 gumpaste-wrapped dowels.

3. Place the gumpaste-wrapped dowel, seam side down, on the work surface and allow to dry for 15 to 20 minutes. Once dry, immediately try to push each dowel out of the paste to make sure the dowel isn't sticking to the gumpaste. If the dowel removes easily, place the dowel back inside the cylinder and let dry for 1 hour. If the dowel is difficult to remove, re-dust the dowel with cornstarch before placing it back inside the cylinder of gumpaste to dry.

LEFT TO RIGHT: *A wooden dowel encased in gumpaste to form a piece of bamboo, a dried bamboo stalk without the wooden dowel, and a completed bamboo stalk with a section ring.*

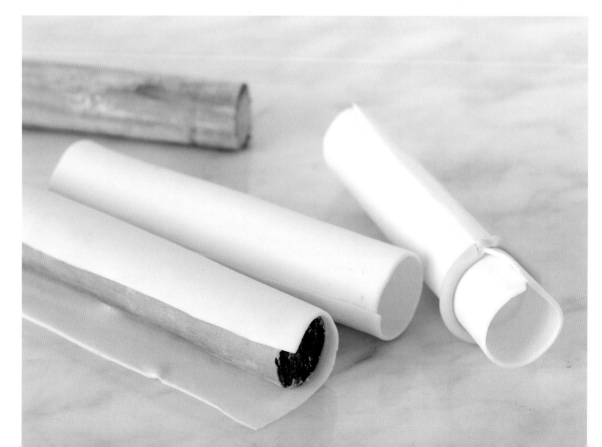

4. After 1 hour, remove each dowel to check again to see that it is not sticking. Re-dust with cornstarch, if necessary, then replace the dowel and let dry for 4 to 5 hours. Once dry, remove the dowel and let the interior of the cylinder dry for several hours or overnight.

SECTION RINGS

1. Place ½ oz (14 g) of gumpaste in a clay gun fitted with the disk with a small round single opening. Push the paste through the opening to extrude a long rounded piece of gumpaste.

2. Cut the gumpaste roll into 3-in (7.6-cm) sections and place randomly around the bamboo with a tiny amount of egg white to give the bamboo a realistic look. Let dry completely for several hours.

AIRBRUSHING

1. You will need green, yellow, and brown airbrush food colors for this project. I like to mix the colors right into the tiny cup that is attached to the gun of the airbrush.

2. Spray each of the bamboo cylinders on its side initially, and then spray some of the cylinders standing upright. For a naturally varied look, spray some of the cylinders with green mixed with a tiny amount of brown color, spray some with yellow mixed with a tiny amount of green, and spray some with all three colors mixed equally.

3. Let the sprayed cylinders dry overnight.

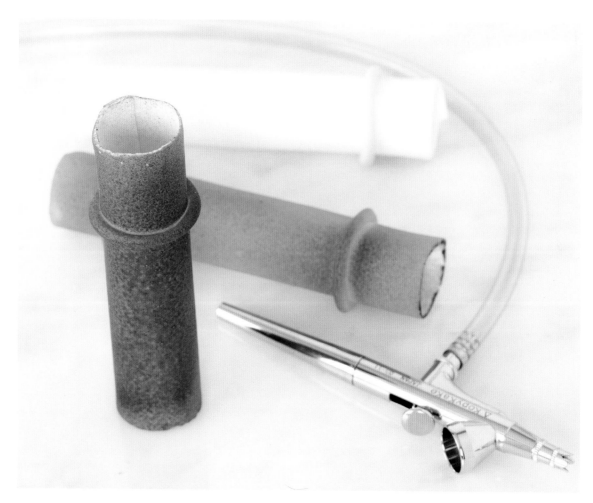

CLOCKWISE FROM TOP: *A completed piece of unsprayed bamboo, an airbrush, a completed piece of bamboo with dark green coloring, and a completed piece of bamboo with light yellow-green coloring.*

Leaves and Spiral Foliage

1. Roll out green gumpaste for making leaves. See page 29 for instructions on making cutter leaves. Cut out about a dozen small leaves with a small rose leaf cutter. Wire the leaves with a 28-gauge green florist wire.

2. See page 31 for instructions on making spiral foliage. You will need about a half-dozen spirals for this cake.

Assembly

1. Attach each piece of bamboo to the side of the cake, seam side in, with royal icing. Place each piece of bamboo as close to the previous piece as possible, leaving as little a space as possible. Continue attaching the bamboo stalks until you have gone completely around the cake.

2. Attach spiral foliage around the cake in several sections, and wrap leaves around the spirals for a dramatic look. Add some leaves around the top of the bamboo.

3. If desired, cut out a leaf-shaped name tag plaque and attach to the cake in between the bamboo stalks.

THE INSPIRATION

IN CREATING THIS DESIGN, I was inspired by a similar design I did many years ago when I competed in a cake competition. The theme for the competition was "the bride's in the clock." For that event, I created a marzipan bear bride, hiding from her husband, to be inside a clock. This antique clock can be used on its own, as shown here, or could be placed as an ornament on top of a square or rectangular groom's cake.

THE CAKE

This is a three-dimensional clock that stands approximately 8 in (20.3 cm) high and about 6½ in (16.5 cm) wide. The clock has a clock face with dials, a door that you can slightly see through, a pendulum, and a door handle, all made from gumpaste. The clock is airbrushed with red and brown airbrush colors mixed together.

THE TECHNIQUES

Clock Panels

1. Trace the patterns for all of the panels of the clock (see Appendix, pages 210–214), including the front and back of the clock (Panels A and B), the sides and bottom of the clock (Panels D, E, and F), the panel under the arch with the hole for the pendulum (Panel G), the clock hands and face, and the clock door frame. (Panel C, which is the curved panel that sits on the top of the clock, should not be cut out until all of the other pieces have dried for about 24 hours on one side and an additional 24 hours on the opposite sides; see Panel C on page 101).

2. Roll out a rectangular piece of gumpaste to about ¼ in (6 mm) thick on a surface lightly coated with shortening. Place the patterns directly on top of the gumpaste and carefully cut out the panels with an X-acto knife or a pizza wheel. Carefully move the cut-out panels to a surface where they will not be disturbed and let dry for 24 hours. After 24 hours, carefully turn the panels over and let dry on the opposite side for an additional 24 hours.

3. When dry, sand each piece with fine sandpaper.

The Pendulum

1. Trace the pattern for the pendulum (see Appendix, page 214). Place a 2-in (5.8-cm) ball of gumpaste into the palm of your hands and shape into a rounded ball. Slightly flatten the ball of paste and place it into the pattern to make sure you have the correct size.

TOP TO BOTTOM: *A small piece of gumpaste in the center of a skewer, a completed pendulum, and a completed pendulum with the arm attached that has been gilded.*

2. For the pendulum arm, cover a 4-in (10-cm) skewer with gumpaste and let dry for several hours. Once the arm is dried, insert it into the pendulum about ½ in (1.3 cm) deep and allow to dry for 24 hours.

3. Once it is dry, gild the pendulum and arm with a small amount of gold powder and a tiny amount of lemon extract, mixed with a #1 sable paintbrush. Use the same paintbrush to brush the gold liquid onto the pendulum and the arm of the pendulum. Let dry for 1 hour.

Door Frame Lattice

1. After sanding the clock door frame, airbrush one side of the frame with a mixture of 3 parts red to 1 part brown airbrush colors. Let dry for 24 hours.

2. Once dry, turn the frame over and place it on a piece of plastic wrap that is taped to a small piece of cardboard. Pipe lattice lines using a #2 round tip with 1 Tbsp (14 g) of Egg White Royal Icing. See page 19 for instructions on piping lattice lines. Let dry overnight and set aside.

Clock Face and Hands

1. Gild the clock face using the same technique as for the pendulum and let dry for several hours.

2. With a #2 round tip and 1 Tbsp (14 g) of Egg White Royal Icing, freehand pipe the clock numbers 12, 3, 6, and 9 in their appropriate clock positions about ½ in (1.3 cm) in from the edge of the clock face. Let dry for a couple of hours. When dry, gild the clock numbers and let dry for 1 hour.

3. Outline the clock hands with a #2 round tip and Egg White Royal Icing and flood the clock hands with flood icing. Let dry. When dry, gild the clock hands and let dry for a couple of hours.

4. Position the hands on the clock face, attaching them with a dot of royal icing.

Backdrop for Clock Face

1. Roll out 2 oz (57 g) of mint green gumpaste to slightly larger than the clock face and about ⅛ in (3 mm) thick on a surface lightly coated with shortening. Use a fluted cutter to cut out the paste. Let dry for 8 hours on one side and then 8 hours on the opposite side.

2. Place the clock face and hands on this fluted backdrop, attaching them with a small amount of royal icing.

Panel C

1. Trace the pattern for Panel C (see Appendix, page 212). Roll out a rectangular piece of gumpaste on a surface lightly coated with shortening, place the pattern on top, and cut out using the same technique as for the other clock panels above. Allow to dry for 5 minutes, and then immediately attach it to the clock (see below).

Clock Shell

1. Paint a line of egg whites with a #1 sable paintbrush around the top curve of Panel A, the back of the clock. Attach Panel C to the top curve of Panel A. Place small objects in front and in back of the curve to hold it together. Let dry for several hours.

2. Check to make sure the curve is secured. Take a small amount of Flood Icing and brush it onto the inside seam of the curve to further secure the curve to the back of the clock. This side will not be seen when the clock is completed.

3. Attach Panel G to the curve. This panel should go from the left edge of the back of the clock to the right edge, and will hold the pendulum's arm. Secure the ends of the curved piece with royal icing. Press firmly but carefully. Allow to dry for several hours.

4. Attach Panels D, E, and F with royal icing. These panels complete the shape of the bottom of the clock. Pipe 1 Tbsp (14 g) of Egg White or Meringue Powder Royal Icing on the inside seam with a #2 round tip and attach the panels. Attach Panel D to the left side edge of Panel G and fit it on the inside edge of Panel A. Join Panel E to the edge of Panel D and set it on the inside of Panel A. Join Panel F to Panel E, fitting it on the inside of Panel A and gluing it to the opposite side of Panel G. Adjust the size of the panels, if needed, by sanding them or scoring with an X-acto knife and breaking off any excess. Place small objects in front and back of the side panels to hold them in place. Allow to dry for 24 hours.

5. Airbrush the clock's shell interior with 3 parts red to 1 part brown airbrush colors. Let dry overnight. Airbrush the exterior of the clock's shell with the same colors. Let dry for 24 hours.

6. Airbrush the clock's front, Panel B, with the same colors. Only the front side of this panel needs airbrushing. The back will be attached to the clock's shell. Let dry for 24 hours.

Assembly

1. To attach the pendulum inside the clock's shell, push the arm of the pendulum through the opening of Panel G. Once the arm is through the opening, secure it with a small amount of gumpaste mixed with a tiny amount of egg white. Let dry for 12 hours to make sure the pendulum holds its position.

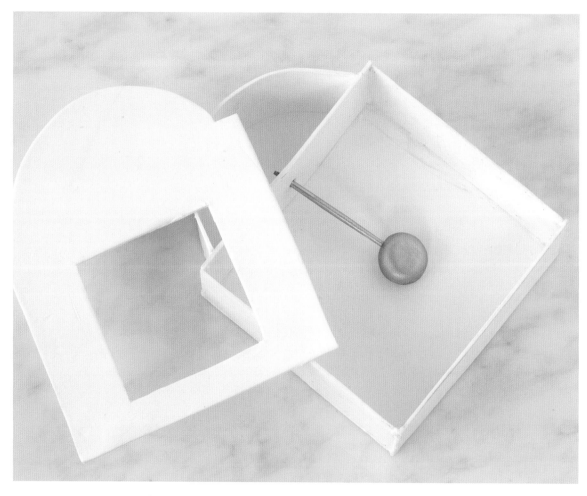

ASSEMBLING THE ANTIQUE CLOCK: *The bottom of the clock fully assembled with the pendulum in place, and the top panel to be attached.*

2. Pipe a line of royal icing with a #2 round tip and 1 Tbsp (14 g) of Egg White or Meringue Powder Royal Icing on top of the clock's shell and on top of Panel G. Before the icing dries, attach the front of the clock, Panel B, to the clock's shell. Let dry for several hours.

3. Attach the clock's face to the front of the clock with a small amount of royal icing.

4. Carefully peel away the door frame from the plastic wrap. Pipe a line of royal icing along the edge of the clock's door frame. Turn the frame over to reveal the right side of the door frame and attach to the front of the clock.

5. Carefully gild the sides of the door frame using the exact same technique as for gilding the pendulum. To finish the frame, use a #2 round tip and 1 Tbsp (14 g) of dark brown colored Egg White or Meringue Powder Royal Icing to pipe a line around the inside edge of the door frame. This will give a finished look to the clock.

6. For the handle, shape a small piece of white gumpaste in the shape of a snail. Let dry for 1 hour and attach to the right side of the door frame with a tiny amount of royal icing. Gild the door handle and let dry for 1 hour.

Wedding cakes are a tradition that goes back as far as the Romans. In late Victorian time, the wedding cake took on a more traditional look with tiers of cakes stacked on top of each other and decorated lavishly with royal icing pipework and decorations. The cakes were more like sugar sculptures. Today, wedding cakes vary widely to reflect the personalities of each couple—from simple buttercream-iced tiers to elaborately decorated cakes, covered in rolled fondant and decorated with lots of sugar flowers and royal icing pipework.

WEDDING CAKES

Crescents and Scroll Cake

THE INSPIRATION

THIS CAKE IS A REFLECTION of my passion for learning the Victorian-style cake art of overpiped scrollwork. I have been inspired by the legendary cake master Joseph Lambeth, who died in the 1940s but whose style of cake artistry lives on through those of us who wish to pursue his passion for precision and three-dimensional cake sculpture. I am one of those students who have pursued this style for more than thirty-five years, and I continue to learn to this day just how you can create a three-dimensional design by piping lines over lines!

THE CAKE

This is an 8-in (20.3-cm) round cake and sits on a 10-in (25.4-cm) board that is 1 in (2.5 cm) high. The cake is covered in deep-colored peach rolled fondant with white and green pipework.

The top and bottom of the cake is lavishly decorated with C scrolls, which have been overpiped several times, as well as overpiped lines under the scrolls. Blossoms, green leaves, and an elevated plaque sit on top with the couple's initials.

The cake could feature an Orange Cream Cake with Orange Curd and an Orange-Infused Buttercream Icing, or a Simnel Cake with French Vanilla Buttercream.

THE TECHNIQUES

Top Edge and Bottom Scrolls

1. Measure the circumference of the cake with adding machine paper. Fold the paper into 8 sections. Measure the top edge of the cake into 8 sections and mark with a stickpin. Measure about 1 in (2.5 cm) up from the bottom of the cake into 8 sections and mark with a stickpin.

2. At the top, pipe drop strings with a #3 round tip and 3 oz (85 g) of Egg White Royal Icing. Position the tip at one of the measured points and apply a burst of pressure. Slowly pull the icing toward you to a distance of about 2 in (5.1 cm) long. Attach the end of the string at the next measured point. Pipe the drop strings from one section to the next, leaving about ¼ in (6 mm) on each side of the drop string. This will give you a ½-in (1.3-cm) space between each drop string. Do the same for the bottom of the cake. Leaving the correct amount of space in between each drop string will be important later when we decorate between the scrolls with leaves and plunger flowers. Let the drop strings dry for 30 minutes.

3. Pipe C scrolls directly over the drop strings with a #3 round tip. To begin the C scroll, slightly touch the drop string with your tip, and apply a careful amount of pressure as you slightly drag the tip over the surface of the drop string, forming a C. Lift the tip slightly and allow the scroll to fall to the drop string. Then, carefully lower the tip to the end of the scroll and touch the surface of the drop string as you end in an opposite C scroll. Continue with the next scroll. Then, do exactly the same for the bottom of the cake.

4. Let dry for 15 minutes, then overpipe the C scrolls again, directly on top of the previous scrolls. Overpipe 5 to 6 C scrolls on the top of the cake and about 3 to 4 C scrolls at the bottom of the cake, letting dry for 15 minutes between each round of scrolls.

5. Position your tip approximately ¼ in (6 mm) below the C scrolls at the top of the cake. Pipe a scallop line, following the shape of the C scrolls. Repeat this for the bottom C scrolls. Let dry for 1 hour.

6. Pipe an additional line below the first scallop line, following the design of the previous line. Repeat this for the bottom. Let dry for 1 hour. Pipe an additional scallop line, slightly below the previous one, for the top and bottom scrolls of the cake. Then add one additional scallop line, only for the top scroll.

7. For the third and fourth scallop lines at the top of the cake, end the scallop line in a V shape with the #3 round tip. This technique gives continuity to the scrolls. For the bottom scrolls, just the third scallop line will end in a V shape.

8. Return to the top scrolls and add additional scallop lines on top of the second and third scallops. Repeat this for the second and third scallops for the bottom scrolls. Then finish each C scroll and scallop line with an additional scroll or line using 2 oz (57 g) of moss green royal icing and the #2 round tip.

BUILDING A C SCROLL, LEFT TO RIGHT: *Piping drop strings, overpiping the drop strings with C scrolls, and a finished section, which includes overpiped lines in descending order and is finished off with green royal icing to provide depth to the scrolls.*

Top Scallop Design

1. Using the top C scrolls as a measuring guide, mark the top of the cake with a stickpin at the center point of each C scroll and about ½ in (1.3 cm) in from the scroll.

2. Pipe curved scallops with a #3 round tip and 3 oz (85 g) of Egg White Royal Icing from one marking to the next. Continue until you have gone completely around the top of the cake. Then overpipe 4 to 5 lines over the scallops with the same #3 round tip, allowing a drying time of 10 to 15 minutes between each overpipe curve.

3. Pipe an additional set of lines inside the first circle of scallop curves, about ¼ in (6 mm) from the outside curve, just like the scallop lines under the C scrolls. Pipe a third line of scallops about ¼ in (6 mm) from the second curve, and then continue by adding a fourth row of scallops. Overpipe the second, third, and fourth curved lines, using one more overpiped line for each row as you progress from the second to the fourth line, to create a "descending" look from high to low.

4. Pipe a finishing line over the inner row of scallops, closest to the center of the cake, with a #2 round tip and moss green royal icing.

Plaque

1. Roll out gumpaste in a deep peach color on a tiny amount of vegetable shortening to about ⅛ in (3 mm) in depth. Trace the gumpaste plaque scroll (see Appendix, page 215) and place the pattern over the gumpaste. Cut carefully with an X-acto knife. Let the panel dry for 24 hours on one side and then an additional 24 hours on the opposite side.

2. Trace the monogram for this plaque (see Appendix, page 215). Then transfer the monogram from the tracing onto the finished plaque using the carbon copy method (see page 15). Pipe over the monogram with moss green royal icing and a #3 round tip.

3. Attach the plaque to the top of the scroll cake and secure with a tiny amount of royal icing. The plaque should fit on top of the row of scalloped curves closest to the center of the cake.

4. Fill in the spaces by attaching plunger flowers with a tiny amount of royal icing and adding gumpaste leaves.

Courtly Dress

THE INSPIRATION

WHAT A DRESS TO WEAR to a fancy costume party! This dress reminds me of a time when I joined an organization called The Society of Creative Anachronism (SCA), which is devoted to researching and recreating the arts of the Middle Ages and the Renaissance. At the SCA's events, attendees would wear courtly garments and the men would don armor to fight for kingship. This dress also brings back a lot of cherished moments spent as a costume-dressed "wench" at the Renaissance Fair in Tuxedo, New York.

THE CAKE

This dress is made up of three tiers. The bottom tier is 7 x 4 in (17.8 x 10 cm), the middle tier is 6 x 1 in (15.2 x 2.5 cm) and the top tier is 4 x 3 in (10 x 7.6 cm). All three tiers are covered in white rolled fondant and then decorated in a dark green rolled fondant. Each section of the dress has lots of detailing. The top of the dress is made up of two panels that are embossed with a textured rolling pin to resemble rich-looking brocade and are attached to the top tier of the cake. The bottom two tiers of the dress are made up of several panels of deep green–colored gumpaste with stitching and side drapes to give the dress a lot of drama. Ropes, medallions, and a white shift accentuate the regal look of the dress.

The cake could be composed of a Devil's Food Cake with a Dark Chocolate Buttercream Icing, or a Victorian Sponge Cake with Lemon-Infused Buttercream Icing.

THE TECHNIQUES

The Dress

1. To create the dress, you will need approximately 3 lb (48 oz or 1,362 g) of a dark green–colored gumpaste, and 1 lb (16 oz or 454 g) of white gumpaste that will be colored later. First, cover all of the tiers with white rolled fondant and let dry overnight. The next day, attach the bottom and middle tiers together with a small amount of royal icing. Attach the bottom two tiers on a 10 in (25.4 cm) round drum that is also covered in rolled fondant.

2. Roll out a piece of dark green gumpaste on a surface that has been lightly oiled with vegetable shortening. Roll the paste about ⅙ in (1.5 mm) thick and use an X-acto knife to cut a panel approximately 9 x 6 in (22.8 x 15.2

LEFT TO RIGHT: *A pleated drape, and attaching the pleated drape to the cake.*

cm). Using the pattern (see Appendix, page 218) as a guide, cut one end of the panel into 4 or 5 equal scallops about ¼ in (6 mm) deep from the edge of one end of the panel. Stitch along the very edge of the scalloped cut with a quilting wheel, and gather the top of the panel into ½-in (1.3-cm) pleats.

3. Pick up the panel and attach it to the bottom two tiers of the cake with a tiny amount of water. Attach the pleated end to the center of the top tier, and drape it down to the cake board. See page 11 for more on working with freehand drapery.

4. Create the next panel using the same technique, and attach it to the cake with a tiny amount of water, slightly overlapping the previous panel to give a full look to the dress. Continue creating and attaching panels until the entire bottom of the dress is completed.

5. To finish the bottom of the dress, place ½ oz (14 g) of dark green gumpaste into a clay gun fitted with a three-whole disk and expel the paste from the clay gun to create a rope approximately 8 in (20.3 cm) long. Attach the rope to the front of the dress with a tiny amount of royal icing.

Side Drapes

1. Color 8 oz (228 g) of the white gumpaste a lighter green or a dusty rose color. Roll out 6 oz (170 g) of paste on a tiny amount of vegetable shortening to approximately 6 x 6 in (15.2 x 15.2 cm) and approximately ⅟₁₆ in (1.5 mm) thick. Cut out 6 strips of paste, each approximately 1 x 6 in (2.5 x 15.2 cm) long.

2. Take one of the strips and brush one edge with a tiny amount of water. Sandwich the strip together, forming a fold for classical drapery, as described on page 12. Repeat to make two or three drapes, and sandwich the drapes together with a tiny amount of water.

3. Attach the double or triple drape to one side of the dress, starting near the front of the dress and draping it to the back. Repeat this process to create another double or triple drape for the opposite side of the dress.

4. Decorate the drapery with rope and tassels, made with the balance of the paste using a clay gun (see pages 14–15).

The Bodice

1. Roll out 3 oz (85 g) of dark green gumpaste to about ⅛ in (3 mm) thick on a surface lightly coated with shortening. Roll a textured rolling pin over the gumpaste to create a brocade fabric-like look. Trace the two bodice patterns (see Appendix, pages 216–217) with parchment paper and place the patterns over the textured paste. Cut out the panels with an X-acto knife and let dry for 15 minutes.

2. Stitch the panels around the edges with a quilting wheel. Use a #5 round tip to cut eyelets into each side of each panel, about ¼ in (6 mm) deep from the edge of the panel and spaced out about ½ in (1.3 cm) down. This will equal 5 or 6 eyelets.

3. Attach the top tier of the cake to the dress with a small amount of royal icing. Attach the V cut panel to the front of the top tier and the straight-back panel to the back with a tiny amount of water. Align the eyelets from the front panel with those on the back panel.

TOP RIGHT: *The front panel of the bodice with the V shape.*
BOTTOM LEFT: *The back panel of the bodice.*

4. Using a PME #0 tip and Egg White Royal Icing, pipe double-stitched lines
to connect the eyelets. Start with the left eyelets, and pipe diagonal crisscross double lines to the right eyelets. Then pipe diagonal crisscross lines
from the right eyelets to the left eyelets.

Medallions and Streamers

1. Roll out ½ oz (14 g) of deep green gumpaste the same color as the bodice of the dress on a surface lightly coated with shortening. Cut out a disk using a large daisy cutter. Take a pea-size piece of green gumpaste and roll it into a ball. Attach to the center of the daisy medallion with a tiny amount of water. Gild the round ball and let dry for 1 hour. This will be used as the medallion for the top center of the bodice.

2. Cut out 4 calyxes from the same green gumpaste using a large rose calyx cutter. Fold the points of each calyx back to create bow-like loops, forming a rounded medallion. Roll out small pea-size balls of green gumpaste and attach one to the center of each rose calyx medallion. Gild the small balls and let dry for 1 hour.

3. For the streamers, color 1 oz (28.4) of the balance of the white gumpaste a medium pink. Roll out the paste and cut out 4 streamers approximately ½ in (1.3 cm) x 3 in (7.62 cm) long on a surface lightly coated with shortening. Fold the streamers in sets of 2 to make 4 streamers.

4. Attach bunches of streamers to the dress, two near the front and two near the bottom of the dress, with a tiny amount of water or royal icing. Then attach a rose calyx medallion on top of each bunch of streamers.

5. Make two 3-in (7.62-cm-)-long ropes using a clay gun and dark green gumpaste (see page 15). Attach the ropes to the front panel of the bodice with a tiny amount of water or royal icing. Attach one end of each rope to the top side of the bodice, extend them down to the front center of the bodice so the two ropes meet at the front center, and gild. Attach the daisy medallion in the center.

Shift (Undergarment)

1. Roll out 2 oz (57 g) of white gumpaste on a tiny amount of vegetable shortening until it is extremely thin and approximately 8 in (20.3 cm) in diameter.

2. Place the circle of paste inside the top of the bodice. Pull the center up and push and tuck the paste through the armholes of the bodice, fluffing up the garment for a more attractive look.

Oriental Stringwork Cake

THE CAKE

This is a two-tiered cake iced in Meringue Powder Royal Icing. The top tier is 7 x 4 in (17.7 x 10 cm) and the bottom tier is 9 x 4 in (22.8 x 10 cm). The cake is decorated with delicate upside-down piping. To achieve this, drop strings are piped right side up around the cake and then the strings are allowed to dry. Then the cake is actually turned upside down and more drop strings are piped. Those strings are allowed to dry, the cake is turned right side up again, and the process continues.

A traditional pound cake that is iced in marzipan and then in Meringue Powder Royal Icing is the key here, as the cake needs to be quite sturdy in order to be turned upside down. If a different flavor of cake is desired, another option would be to ice Styrofoam cakes for display at the wedding and have cut-up cakes in the desired flavor in the back ready to serve.

THE TECHNIQUES

Stringwork

1. Measure the circumference of the top tier of the cake with adding machine paper. Divide the tier into 16 sections (or any even number of sections). Mark the sections with a toothpick and then go back and pipe a small dot over each toothpick mark with a #2 round tip and Egg White Royal Icing. This is called the marker. Let dry for several hours.

2. Fill a paper cone with 1 Tbsp of Egg White Royal Icing and a PME "0" tip. Pipe drop strings from one marker to another. Let dry for 30 minutes. Then carefully turn the cake upside down and pipe drop strings from one marker to another. Let dry for 30 minutes.

3. Turn the cake right side up again and pipe another row of drop strings from one marker to another, slightly lower than the previous drop strings. The second row of strings should be approximately ⅛ in (3 mm) away from the first. Continue around the cake and let dry for 30 minutes. Then turn the cake upside down again and repeat the second row of drop strings from marker to marker. Let dry for 30 minutes.

4. Turn the cake right side up again, and continue the process above until you have 3 sets of drop strings, each about ⅛ in (3 mm) apart from one another, facing right side up and 3 sets facing upside down.

5. Repeat this entire process to create rows of drop strings on the bottom tier.

6. When all the strings are completely dry, attach the top tier on top of the bottom tier and finish with a ribbon.

A cake divided into top and bottom sections using tiny dots of royal icing, and drop strings added from one section to another.

Seasonal celebrations are always treasured moments, and cakes inspired by the seasons provide a gratifying combination of details, colors, and textures. These cakes reflect the memorable experiences that most of us have shared at some point, from holiday gatherings to the warmth of early spring, and each one is special and inspirational, with exciting details and delicious little trinkets!

SEASONAL
CAKES

THE INSPIRATION

WHITE, GREEN, RED, A LITTLE YELLOW, holly berries, and foliage all say one thing. It's time to celebrate a most beloved holiday where gift giving and family togetherness are a tradition. For this cake, the goal was to create something that almost looked like a present, and that could be served at any type of Christmas gathering, from a not-so-formal to a very formal setting.

THE CAKE

This is a 9-in square x 4-in (22.8-cm square x 10-cm)-high cake, iced in white rolled fondant with red and green ribbon strips and set on a square board. The cake has a lovely spray of ivy, holly leaves, berries, and spirals, flanked by ribbons and yellow bells. The cake is composed of a Lemon-Cream Pound Cake with Lemon-Infused Buttercream Icing.

THE TECHNIQUES

Bells

1. Oil a 1½-in to 2-in (3.8-cm to 5.1-cm) bell-shaped mold with a tiny amount of vegetable shortening, and then dust the mold with cornstarch. Remove any excess cornstarch. Knead 2 oz (57 g) of egg yellow gumpaste until pliable. Roll the paste into a round ball and then make a deep indentation in the ball with your thumbs. Place the gumpaste into the bell mold and push with your thumbs, thinning the paste as you push the paste toward the top of the bell mold. Use your thumbs to continue thinning and pressing the gumpaste against the sides of the bell mold.

LEFT TO RIGHT: *Pressing gumpaste into a bell mold, and a finished gumpaste bell.*

2. Cut off any excess gumpaste that extends from the opening of the bell mold. Immediately remove the gumpaste from the mold, to make sure the gumpaste isn't sticking. If it is sticking, re-dust the mold with more cornstarch. Place the gumpaste back into the mold and allow it to dry inside the mold. Remove after 1 hour to check for sticking. Dust with additional cornstarch, if necessary, and place the paste back into the mold, and let dry overnight.

Ribbon Strips

1. Roll out 3 oz of red and green gumpaste to about ⅛ in (3 mm) thick on a surface lightly coated with shortening. Using an X-acto knife, cut out ribbon strips about 2 in (5.1 cm) wide from the green gumpaste and about 1½ in (3.8 cm) wide from the red gumpaste, or vice versa. Cut each strip to a length of 5 to 6 in (12.7 to 15.2 cm).

2. Stitch the edges of each ribbon strip with a quilting wheel and cut the ends of the strips in a V shape. Layer one color over another and attach with a tiny amount of water for a dramatic look.

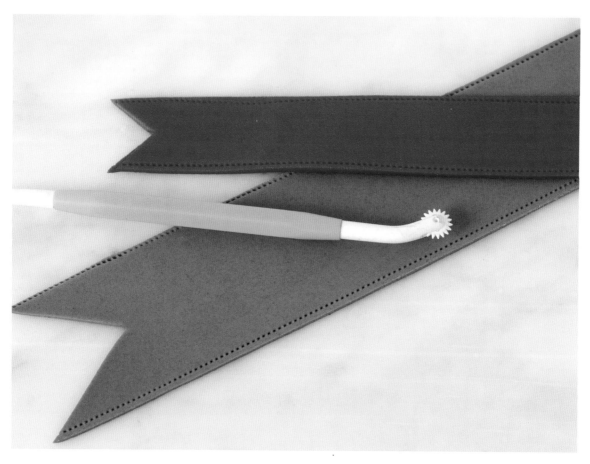

A strip of red ribbon gumpaste layered on top of a green ribbon strip.

Leaves and Berries

1. To make a berry, roll a tiny ball of red gumpaste. Dip a 28-gauge piece of florist wire into a little egg white and insert it into the red ball. Make 30 to 40 berries and tape 9 to 11 berries together as a bunch with a piece of florist tape.

2. Make 24 cutter leaves (see page 29). Bunch them together with sprays of berries and tape with florist tape.

Bountiful!

THE INSPIRATION

BRING IN THE HARVEST with a glorious full-size pumpkin, an ear of corn, peas in a pod, and pumpkin leaves. Nothing feels more comforting than a cup of warm mulled cider and the feeling of fall in the air. The concept for this fall pumpkin cake was easy, but the execution of the pumpkin turned out to be a challenge. First I decided to cover the round sphere with an extremely large piece of rolled fondant, but even after several tries, the paste just did not lie correctly. Next, I tried cutting strips of fondant to attach to the sphere, which worked much better—now, I am a lover of pumpkins!

THE CAKE

This is a 9-in (22.8-cm) sphere that is iced with buttercream icing and then covered in strips of orange rolled fondant. The cake is baked in two half-sphere pans and sandwiched together. The pumpkin is placed on a square board and surrounded by late summer vegetables to complete the "harvest bounty" theme. The cake is composed of a Banana-Rum Cake with Orange-Infused Buttercream Icing.

THE TECHNIQUES

Pumpkin

1. Knead 2 lb (32 oz or 908 g) of orange rolled fondant until pliable. Trace the pumpkin strip pattern (see Appendix, page 219).

2. Roll out 4 oz (114 g) of the orange paste onto a tiny amount of vegetable shortening to the length of the pumpkin strip pattern and about ⅛ in (3 mm) thick. Place the pattern over the strip and cut the shape out with an X-acto knife. Carefully remove the paste and attach it to the pumpkin, starting at the top center of the pumpkin and smoothing the panel down the side and just slightly under the pumpkin.

3. Continue to roll out 4 oz (114 g) of orange fondant at a time and repeat the process, making sure that the strips are placed as close to each other as possible. As you continue to attach panel strips, you may need to do a little bit of adjusting of the panels to get them to fit closely together all the way around the pumpkin.

LEFT TO RIGHT: *Cutting a pumpkin panel from a pattern, an airbrushed panel, and several airbrushed panels attached side by side.*

LEFT TO RIGHT: *A walnut-size piece of greenish gumpaste, and a finished hand-shaped and airbrushed stem.*

Stem

Roll 2 oz (57 g) of colored fondant into a ball and then place it on a work surface. Roll the ball into a log, applying more pressure at one end of the log. Pick up the log and begin to hand-shape it to look like a stem. Check the base of the stem by placing it on top of the pumpkin to make sure that it fits.

Calyx and Pumpkin Leaf

1. Roll out a grape-size piece of gumpaste and cut out an extra-large green calyx using a rose calyx cutter. Use a dogbone tool to soften the calyx on a cell pad. Let dry for 2 hours.

2. Roll out ½ oz (14 g) of mint green gumpaste on a surface lightly coated with shortening and cut out two maple leaves freehand, with a cutter, or using a pattern (see Appendix, page 219) as a guide. Use a leaf veiner to add texture to the leaf and soften with a dogbone tool. Let dry for 1 hour.

Airbrushing

1. Airbrush the pumpkin with orange and a tiny amount of brown airbrush food colors, mixed in the airbrush cup. Stand about 12 in (30.4 cm) away from the pumpkin and spray the color mixture over each of the pumpkin's seams.

2. Airbrush the stem with orange, green, and brown airbrush colors, mixed in the airbrush cup.

3. Airbrush the leaf with orange and a tiny amount of green and brown airbrush colors mixed in the airbrush cup.

Corn

1. Hand-shape about 2 oz (57 g) of egg yellow gumpaste by rolling the paste back and forth in the center of your palm, forming a 3½- to 4-in (9.5-cm to 10.2-cm) log. Slightly taper both ends of the log and round off the ends with your thumb and index finger. To give the corn texture, score vertical lines about ¼ in (6 mm) apart with an X-acto knife. Then, score horizontal lines across the vertical lines about ¼ in (6 mm) apart. Airbrush the corn with a tiny amount of lemon yellow and a tiny amount of brown airbrush colors, mixed right in the airbrush cup. Lightly spray the corn with the color.

2. Roll out 1 oz (28 g) of greenish-yellow gumpaste to about ⅛ in (3 mm) thick on a tiny amount of vegetable shortening. Cut out 3 long oval shapes with an X-acto knife. The leaves should be the same length as the corn. See image on page 139 for approximate size and shape.

3. Carefully remove the leaves and place on a surface lightly dusted with cornstarch. Emboss the leaves with a corn husk, which will form lines on the leaves. Attach the leaves, which should now resemble corn husks, to the corn in three strips, gluing the strips with a tiny amount of water. Roll back the top edge of the leaves, to reveal the actual corn inside the corn husk. Airbrush the corn husk with a tiny amount of yellow and green airbrush colors, mixed right in the airbrush cup. Lightly spray the corn husk, toward the bottom of the corn.

Peas

1. For the pod, roll out 1 oz (28 g) of mint green gumpaste on a tiny amount of vegetable shortening. Roll the paste about ⅛ in (3 mm) thick. Cut out a narrow oval shape with an X-acto knife, about 3½ to 4 in (9.5 to 10.2 cm) long, using the same technique as for cutting a freehand leaf. Let dry lengthwise for 1 hour over a long narrow dowel. This will form the pod for the peas.

2. Take the balance of the paste left over from making the pod and hand-roll about 6 or 7 pea-size balls of mint green gumpaste. Let dry for 30 minutes.

3. To assemble, remove the pod from the dowel. Attach the peas on the inside of the pod with a tiny dot of Meringue Powder Royal Icing.

Assembly

1. Attach the calyx on top of the pumpkin with a tiny amount of royal icing. Place a tiny amount of royal icing on top of the calyx and attach the stem.

2. Attach one leaf at the top of the pumpkin near the stem, and place another leaf at the base of the pumpkin.

3. Place the corn and peas in the pod around the base of the pumpkin to finish the cake.

Spring Love

THE INSPIRATION

THIS CHARMING CAKE spells out the spring love theme with a heart-shaped spiral and a lovely spray of spring flowers, including cherry blossoms, buds, foliage, and ribbons. The pretty floral painting of leaf green and soft pinks combined with the yellow-green fondant evokes emotion and adds to the romance of this spring love cake.

THE CAKE

This is an 8-in (20.3-cm) round cake that sits on a 12-in (30.4-cm) cake board, and both are covered in yellow-green rolled fondant. The cake has painted leaves and sugar blossoms that extend from the cake board all the way up to the top edge of the cake. A beautiful heart-shaped spiral sits on top of the cake with pretty ribbons tied around it, and a lovely spray of spring flowers sits just inside the heart-shaped spiral. The cake could be composed of a Cream Cheese Pound Cake with an Almond-Vanilla Buttercream Icing, or a Banana-Rum Cake with Swiss Meringue Buttercream.

THE TECHNIQUES

Painting

1. To create the simple painting of leaves and forget-me-nots on the sides of the cake, assemble a small dish with two dots of leaf green gel food color, one dot of a pinkish gel food color, and two to three dots of liquid whitener. You will also need a #1 sable paintbrush and a glass of water to clean your brush.

2. Blend some of the leaf green food color with a little of the liquid whitener. This will create a more pastel green tone. Keep some of the green color separate, without liquid whitener, to use for the branches of the leaves.

3. Starting at the cake board, hold your paintbrush at a 90° angle. Apply a little pressure with your paintbrush and paint a thin wavy line using the green without liquid whitener. This will be your branch. The branch can be any length. Extend the branch up onto the side of the cake.

4. Using the green with liquid whitener added to it, position your paintbrush at any point on the branch. Touch the branch and begin to pull the brush toward you, easing off the pressure as you complete a leaf. The leaves should be about 1 to 1¼ in (2.5 to 3.2 cm) long. Continue to paint leaves in various directions.

LEFT TO RIGHT: *Painted lines which resemble branches, and painted lines decorated with painted dots and plunger flowers.*

5. Wash your brush, and mix a little liquid whitener in the pinkish gel food color. To paint flowers among the leaves, dip the tip of your brush in the pinkish color and paint 5 symmetrical dots in a bunch. Paint a dot of the liquid whitener in the center of the bunch to finish the flower.

Cherry Blossoms

MAKING THE STAMENS

1. Wrap a piece of cotton thread 10 times around your index and middle fingers together. Cut the excess thread and carefully remove the ring of thread from your fingers.

2. Make a hook at one end of each of two 28-gauge white or green florist wires. Place each hooked end on opposing sides of the ring of thread—that is, at the 12 o'clock and 6 o'clock positions. Close both hooks to secure the wires to the thread. Carefully pick up the two wires and cut the thread down the middle, making two sets of stamens.

3. Tape the hook part of each wire and the end of the thread that is held by the hook with florist tape to secure the thread to the wire. The thread should be no longer than ½ in (1.3 cm). Trim with scissors if necessary.

4. Dust the thread with daffodil yellow petal dust. Dip the ends of the thread in egg whites and then in cosmos (pinkish) petal dust to form pollen. Set aside.

MAKING THE BLOSSOMS

1. Color 1 oz (28 g) of gumpaste a soft pink color. Wrap in plastic until ready to use and place it in an airtight container. To make a rounded skewer for shaping the petals, cut the pointed end of a wooden skewer with a pair of heavy-duty scissors, making it 5 to 6 in (12.7 to 16.5 cm) long. Use sandpaper to soften both ends of the skewer, rounding the ends and removing the hard edge. You will use this tool to soften, stretch, and mark lines on the petals.

2. For each blossom, shape a pea-size bit of pink gumpaste into a cone. Insert the rounded skewer into the paste and make 5 equally spaced slits with an X-acto knife. This is the same technique used for making a basic five-petal blossom (see page 26).

3. Put a little cornstarch on your index finger and carefully place the unshaped flower on it. Hold the trumpet part of the flower with your thumb. With your writing hand, place the modeling stick on top of one of the florets. Starting at the center of the floret, rotate the stick back and forth with your thumb and index finger, stretching the petal. Then pull the stick across the petal to round its edges. Shape each petal using this technique.

4. Insert a wire with stamens through the center of the flower. Brush egg white on the florist tape before it enters the cavity of the flower and carefully rotate the trumpet with your index finger and thumb to secure it to the wire. Allow to dry on Styrofoam.

5. To dust the cherry blossom, brush cosmos (pinkish) petal dust on the inside edge of each petal. Brush moss green petal dust on the trumpet end.

Leaves and Buds

See pages 25–31 for instructions on making leaves and buds.

Spiral Heart

See page 31 for instructions on making spirals. Make several spirals, then twist them together to extend the length of the wires. Hand-shape this long, wired piece into a heart shape. Tie ribbons in the color of your choice around the heart-shaped spiral for a more decorative look.

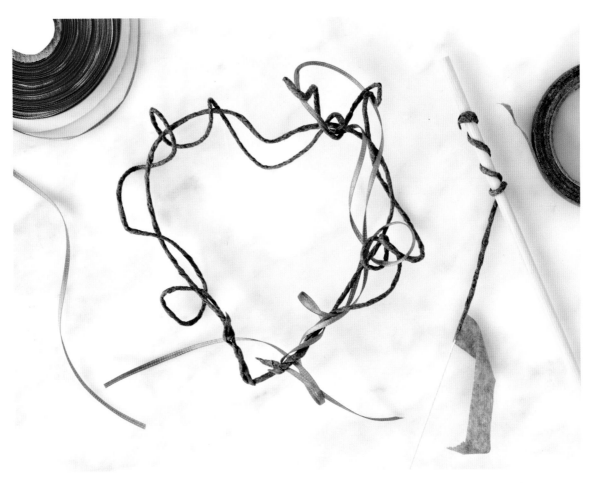

Large taped spirals hand-shaped into a heart shape, with additional spirals and ribbons intertwined.

Decorated cookies and cupcakes are the "now" thing in confectionery art. They are small and complete, a personal individualized serving, and they are affordable, for the most part. They have become a phenomenal industry all unto their own, perhaps because everyone can identify with a cupcake or a cookie. They're a quick, scrumptious, and immediately satisfying indulgence!

Beautifully decorated cookies have become popular among brides and grooms as a wedding favor for guests to take home. Exquisitely boxed and tied with beautiful ribbons, these tiny little treasures become a lasting tribute to the devoted couple.

Cupcakes also continue to be popular around the world. These tiny morsels can be seen everywhere, from posh weddings in place of the traditional wedding cake, to children's functions—especially birthdays—to the finest bakeries and even television competitions. Cupcakes were initially meant to be simple and easy to eat, but these days many are quite decorative and decadent; from swirls and sprinkles to elaborate three-dimensional figures piped or sculpted in buttercream and rolled icings. Whether they are simple or complex, though, cupcakes should always be delicious and easy to eat in a few bites.

SMALL BITES
DECORATED COOKIES AND CUPCAKES

When a Cookie Isn't Just a Cookie

THE INSPIRATION

A DECORATED COOKIE is truly "more than just a cookie." I borrowed this phrase from my friend and colleague Cheryl Kleinman. We once co-chaired an event at Bakers Dozen East in New York where we assembled many cookie decorating authors and artists. She coined this phrase and I never forgot it! A decorated cookie can be a work of art, so much so that it's hard to eat or part with.

The designs for these cookies are based on my classical style of cake decorating. I enjoy creating confections with clean lines, a soft color palette, embroidery, pipework, and lots of attention to details. These cookies represent a style of cake artistry that's old, yet refined and delicate—perhaps more influenced by the Australian style than by any other particular style of decorating.

These cookies are sweet, elegant, and artfully designed, and ultimately, designed to be enjoyed!

THE COOKIES

A variety of techniques and cookie and icing recipes were used to create these eye-catching morsels. Practically all of the techniques used here can be found in "The Essentials" chapter (pages 7–31). Artfully placed pieces of ribbon on some cookies help to tie the look together.

These cookies feature a wide range of flavors, including almond paste cookies, butter cookies, lemon or orange cream cookies, and chocolate cookies. They are iced with rolled fondant, colored white modeling chocolate, and dark modeling chocolate. A few of the double-decker cookies were sandwiched with ganache, and the dome-shaped cookie is filled with ganache.

THE TECHNIQUES

Dome Cookie

1. Select an acrylic or plastic half-sphere mold the same diameter as the cookie you are going to decorate. For the cookie shown here, a 2½-in (6.3-cm) diameter plastic sphere was used.

2. Roll out some pinkish rolled fondant about 5 in (12.7 cm) in diameter and about ⅛ in (3 mm) thick. Brush the mold with a tiny amount of white vegetable shortening and then dust the mold with a light coating of cornstarch. Fit and shape the rolled fondant into the mold, pressing the paste against the mold with your thumb and middle finger. Immediately take the paste out of the mold to check and see if the paste is sticking to the mold. Re-insert the shaped paste into the mold and continue pressing the paste against the mold. Remove the paste again and check to see if the paste is sticking. Re-dust the mold with cornstarch, if necessary. Place the paste into the mold a third time. This time, let the paste rest in the mold for 24 hours.

3. After 24 hours, cut the excess paste that extends from the mold and gently tamp the mold to release the dome-shaped paste. Let the paste rest for an additional 24 hours to ensure that it is fully dry.

4. Brush a round, 2½- to 3-in (6.3- to 7.6-cm) cookie with light corn syrup. Roll out 2 oz (57 g) dark modeling chocolate to a thickness of about ⅛ in (3 mm). Cut the modeling chocolate with a round or fluted cookie cutter the same diameter as the cookie and place the cut-out chocolate paste onto the cookie.

5. Brush the perimeter of the cookie with a tiny amount of water. This will act as glue when you place the dome-shaped fondant on top. Pipe a large rosette of dark chocolate ganache in the middle of the cookie, then carefully place the dome-shaped fondant on top of the cookie, making sure the edge of the dome is secured to the cookie with additional water, if necessary.

6. Decorate with ribbons, plunger flowers, and some freehand embroidery piping.

Round Chocolate Fan Cookie and Upright Heart-Shaped Cookie

This is a double-decker or two-tiered cookie, with a round fan cookie base and a heart-shaped iced cookie standing upright on top.

1. To create the fan-shaped base, brush a round cookie lightly with corn syrup and set aside. Roll out dark modeling chocolate to about ⅛ in (3 mm) thick on a tiny amount of cornstarch. Place the chocolate between the top and bottom of a fan press. Press firmly. Carefully remove the embossed chocolate and cut out a round shape the same diameter as the cookie. Lightly place the dark modeling chocolate on top of the corn syrup–glazed cookie. Set aside.

2. To create the heart shape, brush a heart-shaped cookie lightly with corn syrup and set aside. Roll out dark modeling chocolate to about ⅛ in (3 mm) thick on a tiny amount of cornstarch. Cut out a heart shape the same size as the heart-shaped cookie. Place the dark modeling chocolate on top of the corn syrup–glazed cookie. Decorate the cookie with plunger flowers and some royal icing embroidery pipework (see pages 10 and 9).

A fan-shaped textured piece of modeling chocolate, and the press used to create the texture.

3. To assemble, mix a tiny amount of dark modeling chocolate with a little water. This will make a sticky paste. Place a small amount of the sticky paste in the center of the fan-shaped rolled chocolate cookie. Place the heart-shaped cookie on top where the sticky chocolate glue is placed. Prop up the heart-shaped cookie with a small, lightweight object and let dry for several hours. When dry, decorate around the sticky paste with plunger flowers and chocolate leaves.

Textured Iced Cookie

1. The icing on this cookie is made using a lace-textured press. First, brush the un-iced cookie with a tiny amount of light corn syrup and set aside. Roll out dark modeling chocolate to ⅛ in (3 mm) thick. Place the modeling chocolate between the lace press and press firmly. Remove the chocolate from the press.

2. Cut out the icing using the same cutter that was used to cut the cookie. Place the icing carefully onto the corn syrup–glazed cookie.

A heart-shaped textured piece of modeling chocolate, and the press used to create the texture.

Oh, Cupcakes!

THE INSPIRATION

MY INSPIRATION FOR THESE CUPCAKES comes from my beginner cake decorating class that focuses on buttercream piping skills. I wanted to show that beautiful cupcakes can be relatively approachable to decorate, using basic piping skills. Since I also teach marzipan modeling in that class, I wanted to show how you can create a more three-dimensional cupcake by using these quick confections!

THE CUPCAKES

Cupcakes should be beautiful and can be decorative, but they must also be palatable, down to the last piece of décor. These cupcakes are upscale and appealing to the eye, but also delicious. My favorite cupcakes are chocolate fudge, almond paste, and yellow cupcakes, with lots of buttercream icings in decorative designs, such as piped rosettes, leaf designs, sweet pea clusters, marzipan berries and fruits, and of course, chocolate, chocolate, chocolate.

THE TECHNIQUES

Cupcake with Piped Rosettes

1. Fill a pastry bag with a #18 star tip and 4 to 6 ounces (114 to 170 g) of Decorator's, Dark Chocolate, or French Vanilla Buttercream icing. Pipe a circular row of rosettes around the edge of the cupcake, at a 45° angle. Pipe another row inside the first row, and continue piping additional rows until you reach the center of the cupcake.

2. For leaves, fill a small paper cone with a #352 leaf tip and load 1 Tbsp (14 g) of moss green buttercream icing. Pipe leaves around the edge of the cupcake, and between the negative spacing not filled in by the piped rosettes.

Basket-weave Cupcake

1. Fill a pastry bag with a #48 basket-weave tip and 4 to 6 ounces (114 to 170 g) of Decorator's, Dark Chocolate, or French Vanilla Buttercream icing. At a 45° angle to the top of the cupcake, pipe a vertical line of icing. This is the downstroke. Now pipe a crossover stroke, starting near the top of the downstroke. Extend the crossover stroke over the downstroke about ¼ in (6 mm). Pipe another crossover stroke, leaving a space the same size as the width of the crossover stroke. This is called the tip space. Continue until you have reached the end of the downstroke. Return to the top of the cupcake and pipe another downstroke, slightly crossing over the ends of the crossover stroke. Then, reposition the tip at the tip space and pipe crossover strokes down the length of the downstroke.

2. Finish the basket weaving with piped leaves using a #352 tip and chocolate buttercream, around the edge of the basket weave, and complete the decorating with gumpaste plunger flowers (see page 10).

Cupcake with Sweet Pea Clusters

1. Fill a pastry bag with a #104 petal-shape tip and 4 to 6 ounces (114 to 170 g) of Decorator's, Dark Chocolate, or French Vanilla Buttercream icing.

2. Hold the tip and pastry bag at a 45° angle to the outside edge of the cupcake, with the wide end touching. Apply a burst of pressure, allowing some icing to flow through the tip. Drag the tip to the surface of the cupcake as you pull the tip toward yourself. Angle the back of the tip up as you ease the pressure and stop. This is called a flute.

3. Position the tip at the upper left- or right-hand side of the flute, with the wide end of the tip touching the surface. Slightly angle the tip to a 45° angle. Apply a burst of pressure as you drag the tip to the tail end of the

flute. Stop the pressure and pull the tip toward you. Now position the tip at the opposite side of the flute and repeat the squeeze-and-pull technique. You now have a small sweet pea cluster. Continue piping sweet pea clusters around the edge of the cupcake.

4. Pipe the next layer of clusters inside the first layer and continue until you reach the center.

5. Fill in the negative spacing with moss green buttercream icing, piped with a #352 leaf tip.

Cupcake with Marzipan Raspberries

1. Hand-shape 3 oz (85 g) of red marzipan into small balls. Roll the balls onto a cheese grater to add texture. Add a center cavity to each textured ball with a serrated marzipan tool. Let dry.

2. Ice the cupcake with a small amount of Decorator's, Dark Chocolate, or French Vanilla Buttercream icing, using a small offset spatula. Attach the marzipan berries, starting at the outer edge of the cupcake and working your way toward the center.

3. Heat equal parts water and light corn syrup together, and brush the syrup over the marzipan berries. This will add a shine to the berries.

4. Complete the cupcake by piping leaves into the negative spacing, using moss green buttercream icing and a #352 leaf tip.

Cupcake with Marzipan Fruit

1. Color 1 oz (28.3 g) each of green, orange, and brown marzipan.

2. To make a marzipan apple, take a grape-size piece of moss green marzipan and roll it into a round ball. Place the ball of paste in the center of your nondominant hand. Place the middle finger of your dominant hand on top of the paste and move your finger back and forth, applying pressure at one end of the round ball. This will taper one end of the ball and make it smaller than the other end. Place the ball on a work surface with the tapered end down. Make a cavity at the top center of the paste about ¼ in (6 mm) deep with a cone and serrated tool. Shape the apple with your fingers and place a tiny clove into the center of the cavity to complete the apple.

3. To make a marzipan pear, take a slightly larger grape-size piece of brownish-yellow marzipan and roll it into a round ball. Place the ball of paste in the center of your nondominant hand. Place the middle finger of your dominant hand on top of the paste and move your finger back and forth, applying pressure at one end of the round ball. This will taper one end of the ball and make it smaller than the other end. Place the rounded end of the ball on a work surface. Position your left and right index fingers halfway down the length of the pear. Apply pressure by moving both fingers back and forth to create a Bosc pear–like shape. Then, take a rounded toothpick and press the toothpick slightly up the rounded end of the pear, forming an indentation. Continue this indentation under the pear and slightly up the rounded end of the opposite side. Place a tiny clove off center at the top of the pear to complete the look.

4. To make a marzipan orange, take a grape-size piece of orange marzipan and roll it into a round ball. Roll the ball of orange paste over a cheese grater to texture it, using your middle finger to rotate the paste back and forth. Then, place the textured ball of paste back into the center of your

nondominant hand and, using the middle finger of your dominant hand, slightly soften the textured paste by rolling it back and forth. Place a tiny clove at the top center of the ball and bury the clove until it is flush with the skin of the orange paste.

5. Hand-shape enough miniature apples, oranges and pears for the top of the cupcake, and set aside to dry.

6. Ice the cupcake with a small amount of Decorator's, Dark Chocolate, or French Vanilla Buttercream icing, using a small offset spatula. Arrange the marzipan fruit on the cupcake.

7. Heat equal parts water and light corn syrup together and brush over the marzipan fruit to add shine.

8. Pipe leaves into the negative spacing using moss green icing and a #352 leaf tip.

9. To make a handle, color 1 oz (28.3 g) of white modeling chocolate green and place into a clay gun with the scalloped disk. Extrude the paste from the gun and cut off a piece 4 in (10 cm) long. Hold the paste at both ends and twist in opposite directions to form a rope shape. Let the rope dry on a curved surface for several hours. Once dried, make two cavities in the cupcake and place the handle ends in the cavities. Secure with buttercream icing.

THE
RECIPES

Traditional Pound Cake

EQUIPMENT: 5- or 6-qt mixer
PAN SIZE: Two 10 x 2 in (25.5 x 5)
YIELD: Two 10 in x 2-in (25.5 x 5-cm) round cake layers
BAKING TIME: 50 to 55 minutes

12 oz (340 g) unsalted butter

1¼ lb (20 oz or 567 g) granulated sugar

6 large eggs

8 oz (228 g) sour cream

2 tsp (10 ml) pure vanilla extract

1 tsp (5 ml) lemon extract

12 oz (340 g) cake flour

½ tsp (2 g) baking soda

¼ tsp (.5 g) mace

½ tsp (2.5 g) salt

6 oz (177 ml or 170 g) buttermilk

PREHEAT the oven to 325°F (163°C). Spray the cake pans with nonstick cooking spray and line the bottoms of the pans with parchment paper.

IN the bowl of a stand mixer fitted with the paddle attachment, cream the butter and sugar together for 5 minutes on medium speed. Stop and scrape down the bowl. Cream for 1 minute more, and scrape down the bowl again.

ADD the eggs one at a time to the creamed butter and sugar mixture. Mix thoroughly after each addition.

ADD the sour cream, vanilla and lemon extracts and mix for 2 minutes on slow to medium speed, continuously scraping down the bowl.

IN a medium bowl, sift together the cake flour, baking soda, mace, and salt. Add the dry ingredients to the wet ingredients in the mixer bowl, alternately with the buttermilk, in 3 increments, mixing thoroughly after each addition.

POUR the batter into the prepared pans and bake until a toothpick inserted in the center comes out clean.

Orange Cream Pound Cake

EQUIPMENT: 5- or 6-qt mixer

PAN SIZE: Two 10 x 2 in (25.5 x 5 cm)

YIELD: Two 10 x 2-in (25.5 x 5-cm) round cake layers

BAKING TIME: 45 to 50 minutes

1 lb (454 g) cake flour

1 lb (454 g) granulated sugar

1 Tbsp plus 1½ tsp (18 g) baking powder

1 tsp (5 g) salt

8 oz (228 g) unsalted butter, softened

5 oz (148 ml or 140 g) concentrated orange juice

1 Tbsp (15 ml) orange extract

Grated zest of 1 large orange

6 large eggs

8 fl oz (237 ml or 228 g) heavy cream

PREHEAT the oven to 350°F (177°C). Spray the cake pans with nonstick cooking spray and line the bottoms of the pans with parchment paper.

IN the bowl of a stand mixer fitted with the paddle attachment, mix the flour, sugar, baking powder, and salt for 2 minutes on stir speed to sift and blend the dry ingredients.

ADD the butter, concentrated orange juice, orange extract, and orange zest and beat on low speed for 1 minute. Stop and scrape down the bowl. Beat for 2 minutes on medium-high speed. Stop and scrape down the bowl and beat for 1 minute more.

IN a medium bowl, whisk together the eggs and heavy cream. Add to the batter in 3 increments, mixing on low speed. Stop and scrape down the bowl, then increase the speed to medium and beat for 2 minutes. Stop, scrape down the bowl, and then beat for 1 minute more.

POUR the batter into the prepared pans and bake until a toothpick inserted in the center comes out clean.

Lemon Cream Pound Cake

EQUIPMENT: 5- or 6-qt mixer

PAN SIZE: Two 10 x 2 in (25.5 x 5 cm)

YIELD: Two 10 x 2-in (25.5 x 5-cm) round cake layers

BAKING TIME: 45 to 50 minutes

1 lb (454 g) cake flour

1 lb (454 g) granulated sugar

1 Tbsp plus 1½ tsp (18 g) baking powder

1 tsp (5 g) salt

8 oz (228 g) unsalted butter, softened

3 oz (89 ml or 85 g) fresh lemon juice

1 Tbsp (15 ml) lemon extract

Grated zest of 2 lemons

6 large eggs

10 fl oz (296 ml or 283 g) heavy cream

PREHEAT the oven to 350°F (177°C). Spray the cake pans with nonstick cooking spray and line the bottoms of the pans with parchment paper.

IN the bowl of a stand mixer fitted with the paddle attachment, mix the flour, sugar, baking powder, and salt for 2 minutes on stir speed to sift and blend the dry ingredients.

ADD the butter, lemon juice, lemon extract, and lemon zest and beat on low speed for 1 minute. Stop and scrape down the bowl. Beat for 2 minutes on medium-high speed. Stop and scrape down the bowl and beat for 1 minute more.

IN a medium bowl, whisk together the eggs and heavy cream. Add to the batter in 3 increments, mixing on low speed. Stop and scrape down the bowl. Increase the speed to medium and beat for 2 minutes. Stop, scrape down the bowl, and then beat for 1 minute more.

POUR the batter into the prepared pans and bake until a toothpick inserted in the center comes out clean.

Silver White Cake

EQUIPMENT: 5- or 6-qt mixer

PAN SIZE: Two 8 x 2 in (20.5 x 5 cm)

YIELD: Two 8 x 2-in (20.5 x 5-cm) round cake layers

BAKING TIME: 35 to 40 minutes

5 oz (148 mL) egg whites (4–5 large egg whites)

12 oz (340 g) granulated sugar

10 oz (283 g) cake flour

8 oz (237 ml or 228 g) buttermilk

3 oz (85 g) unsalted butter

3 oz (85 g) high-ratio shortening

1 Tbsp (12 g) baking powder

1 tsp (5 g) salt

1 tsp (5 ml) almond extract

PREHEAT the oven to 350°F (177°C). Spray the cake pans with nonstick cooking spray and line the bottoms of the pans with parchment paper.

IN the bowl of a stand mixer fitted with the wire whisk, beat the egg whites on high speed until soft peaks form, about 5 minutes. Gradually add 4 oz of the sugar, 2 Tbsp at a time, and beat until the sugar has dissolved and the whites form stiff peaks. Set aside.

TO another mixer bowl fitted with the paddle attachment add the remaining ingredients and mix on low speed until well combined, scraping down the bowl continuously. Beat on high speed for 2 minutes, continuing to scrape down the bowl.

REDUCE the speed to low, add the beaten egg whites, and mix just until combined.

POUR the batter into the prepared pans and bake until a toothpick inserted in the center comes out clean.

Devil's Food Cake

EQUIPMENT: 5- or 6-qt mixer

PAN SIZE: Two 9 x 2 in (23 x 5 cm)

YIELD: Two 9 x 2-in (23 x 5-cm) round cake layers

BAKING TIME: 40 to 45 minutes

12 oz (340 g) cake flour

1 lb (454 g) granulated sugar

1 tsp (4 g) baking soda

5 Tbsp (40 g) Dutch-process cocoa powder

1 tsp (5 g) salt

12 oz (340 g) unsalted butter, softened

4 oz (114 g) semisweet or bittersweet melted chocolate

5 large eggs

9 fl oz (266 ml or 255 g) buttermilk

2 Tbsp (30 ml) chocolate extract

PREHEAT the oven to 325°F (163°C). Spray the cake pans with nonstick cooking spray and line the bottoms of the pans with parchment paper.

IN a medium bowl, sift together the cake flour, sugar, baking soda, cocoa powder, and salt and add to the mixer bowl. Attach the bowl to the mixer fitted with the paddle attachment. Add the butter and mix for 3 minutes on low speed. Increase the speed to the next highest speed and mix for 1 minute. Check to make sure there are no lumps of butter still in the batter. Add the melted chocolate and mix for 3 minutes on low speed. Then mix on the next highest speed for 1 minute more.

IN a medium bowl, whisk together the eggs, buttermilk, and chocolate extract. Add the egg mixture to the batter in the mixer bowl in 4 increments, mixing on medium speed.

POUR the batter into the prepared pans and bake until a toothpick inserted in the center comes out clean.

Victoria Sponge Cake

EQUIPMENT: 5- or 6-quart mixer

PAN SIZE: Two 9 x 2 in (23 x 5 cm)

YIELD: Two 9 x 2-in (23 x 5-cm) round cake layers

BAKING TIME: 60 to 65 minutes

1 lb (16 oz or 454 g) superfine sugar

10 oz (283 g) unsalted butter, softened

6 large eggs

1 lb (454 g) cake flour

1 Tbsp plus 1½ tsp (18 g) baking powder

½ tsp (2.5 g) salt

8 oz (240 ml or 228 g) whole milk

1 Tbsp (15 ml) pure vanilla extract

PREHEAT the oven to 325°F (163°C). Spray the cake pans with nonstick cooking spray and line the bottoms of the pans with parchment paper.

IN the bowl of a stand mixer fitted with the paddle attachment, cream the butter and sugar together on low to medium speed until light and creamy, about 5 minutes. Add the eggs, one at a time, mixing thoroughly after each addition.

IN a separate mixer bowl, sift together the flour, baking powder, and salt. Attach the bowl to the mixer fitted with the paddle attachment and slowly beat the flour mixture on low speed to blend dry ingredients. Do not overmix.

ADD the milk and vanilla and beat on low speed for 2 minutes. Increase the speed to medium-high and beat for 1 minute until the batter is smooth.

POUR the batter into the prepared pans and bake until a toothpick inserted in the center comes out clean.

Simnel Cake

EQUIPMENT: 5- or 6-qt mixer
PAN SIZE: 9 x 3 in (23 x 7.5 cm)
YIELD: One 9 x 3-in (23 x 7.5-cm) round cake layer
BAKING TIME: 1½ to 1¾ hours

10 oz (283 g) unsalted butter, softened

1 tsp (5 ml) pure vanilla extract

1 lb (454 g) granulated sugar

4 large eggs

10 oz (283 g) cake flour

1 Tbsp (12 g) baking powder

1½ tsp (2.2 g) ground cinnamon

¾ tsp (1 g) freshly grated nutmeg

½ tsp (2.5 g) salt

8 fl oz (240 ml or 227 g) whole milk

2 oz (57 g) chopped pecans

2 oz (57 g) golden raisins

2 oz (57 g) chopped dates

14 oz (397 g) almond paste

Confectioners' sugar, as needed

PREHEAT the oven to 325°F (163°C). Spray the cake pan with nonstick cooking spray and line the bottom with parchment paper.

IN the bowl of a stand mixer fitted with the paddle attachment, cream the butter, vanilla, and granulated sugar together for 4 minutes. Stop, scrape down the bowl, and cream for 1 minute more.

ADD the eggs to the creamed mixture, one at a time, mixing well after each addition.

IN a medium bowl, sift together the flour, baking powder, cinnamon, nutmeg, and salt. Add the dry ingredients alternately with the milk to the creamed mixture.

FOLD the chopped pecans, raisins, and dates into the batter by hand.

POUR half of the batter into the prepared baking pan.

KNEAD the almond paste lightly with a small amount of confectioners' sugar. Roll and shape it to a 9-in (22.8-cm) round disk about ¼ in (6 mm) thick. Place the disk directly on top of the cake batter.

POUR the balance of the cake batter on top of the almond paste disk, and carefully smooth the batter with a metal offset spatula. Lift up the pan and let it drop onto the countertop to burst any air bubbles and allow the batter to settle.

BAKE until the cake shrinks slightly from the sides of the pan, and a toothpick inserted in the center comes out clean.

Cream Cheese Pound Cake

EQUIPMENT: 5- or 6-quart mixer
PAN SIZE: Two 9 in x 2 in (23 x 5 cm)
YIELD: Two 9 x 2-in (23 x 5-cm) round cake layers
BAKING TIME: 1 hour

1 lb (454 g) cake flour

1 lb (454 g) granulated sugar

1 Tbsp plus 1½ tsp (18 g) baking powder

½ tsp (2.5 g) salt

4 oz (114 g) unsalted butter, softened

14 oz (397 g) cream cheese, softened

2 oz (59 ml or 57 g) whole milk

4 large eggs

6 oz (177 ml or 170 g) buttermilk

1 tsp (5 ml) pure vanilla extract

PREHEAT the oven to 325°F (163°C). Spray the cake pans with nonstick cooking spray and line the bottoms with parchment paper.

IN the bowl of a stand mixer fitted with the paddle attachment, mix the flour, sugar, baking powder, and salt for 2 minutes on stir speed to sift and blend the dry ingredients.

ADD the softened butter and cream cheese and beat on low speed for 1 minute. Increase the speed to medium-high and beat for 2 minutes. Stop and scrape down the bowl, and beat for 1 minute more.

ADD the milk and beat for 2 minutes on medium speed.

IN a medium bowl, whisk together the eggs, buttermilk, and vanilla. Add the mixture to the batter in 3 increments, mixing on low speed, then increase the speed to medium and mix for 3 minutes more. Stop, scrape down the bowl, and then beat for 1 minute more.

POUR the batter into the prepared pans and bake until a toothpick inserted into the center comes out clean.

Banana-Rum Cake

EQUIPMENT: 5- or 6-qt mixer
PAN SIZE: 9 x 3 in (23 x 7.5 cm)
YIELD: One 9 x 3-in (23 x 7.5-cm) round cake layer
BAKING TIME: 60 to 65 minutes

1 lb (454 g) cake flour

1 lb (454 g) granulated sugar

1 Tbsp plus 1½ tsp (18 g) baking powder

1 tsp (5 g) salt

12 oz (340 g) unsalted butter, softened

3 ripe pureed bananas (1.2 lb including skin)

1 oz banana liqueur

5 large eggs

3 fl oz (89 ml or 85 g) rum

4 fl oz (120 ml or 114 g) whole milk

PREHEAT the oven to 325°F (163°C). Spray the cake pan with nonstick cooking spray and line the bottom with parchment paper.

IN the bowl of a stand mixer fitted with the paddle attachment, mix the flour, sugar, baking powder, and salt for 2 minutes on stir speed to sift and blend the ingredients.

ADD the butter, pureed banana, and banana liqueur and beat on low speed for 1 minute. Stop and scrape down the bowl. Increase the speed to medium-high and beat for 2 minutes. Stop, scrape down the bowl, and beat for 1 minute more.

IN a medium bowl, whisk together the eggs, rum, and whole milk. Add to the batter in 3 increments, mixing on low speed. Stop and scrape down the bowl, then increase the speed to medium and beat for 2 minutes. Stop, scrape the bowl, and then beat for 1 minute more.

POUR the batter into the prepared pans and bake until a toothpick inserted in the center comes out clean.

Almond Paste Cupcakes

EQUIPMENT: 5- or 6-qt mixer

YIELD: 28 to 30 cupcakes

BAKING TIME: 20 to 25 minutes

6 oz (170 g) unsalted butter, softened

4 oz (114 g) almond paste

1 lb (454 g) granulated sugar

4 large eggs

1 tsp (5 ml) almond extract

10 oz (283 g) cake flour

1 Tbsp (16 g) baking powder

½ tsp (2.5 g) salt

8 fl oz (240 ml) whole milk

PREHEAT the oven to 350°F (177°C). Line cupcake pans with paper liners.

IN the bowl of a stand mixer fitted with the paddle attachment, cream the butter, almond paste, and sugar together for 4 minutes. Stop, scrape down the bowl, and cream for 1 minute more.

ADD the eggs to the creamed mixture, one at a time, mixing well after each addition. Beat in the almond extract.

IN a medium bowl sift together the flour, baking powder, and salt. Alternately add the flour mixture and milk to the creamed mixture in the mixer bowl, ending with the dry ingredients. Beat on medium speed until just incorporated.

SPOON or pipe the batter into the paper liners, filling them about two-thirds full. Lift up each pan and let it drop onto the countertop to burst any air bubbles and allow the batter to settle.

BAKE the cupcakes in the center of the oven until the cupcakes shrink slightly and a toothpick inserted in the center of a cake comes out clean.

Chocolate Fudge Cupcakes

EQUIPMENT: 5- or 6-qt mixer

YIELD: 32 cupcakes

BAKING TIME: 20 to 25 minutes

10 oz (283 g) all-purpose flour

10 oz (283 g) granulated sugar

6 oz (170 g) dark brown sugar, packed

4 oz (114 g) Dutch-process cocoa powder

2¼ tsp (9 g) baking soda

1½ tsp (7.5 g) salt

10 fl oz (296 ml or 283 g) buttermilk

8 oz (228 g) unsalted butter, softened

2 large eggs

1½ tsp (7.5 ml) pure vanilla extract

6 oz (170 g) melted semisweet or bittersweet chocolate

PREHEAT the oven to 350°F (177°C). Line cupcake pans with paper liners.

PUT all of the ingredients (except for the chocolate) into the bowl of a stand mixer. Attach the bowl to the mixer fitted with the paddle attachment. Beat for 1 minute on low speed, scraping down the bowl.

BLEND in the melted chocolate and beat for 2 minutes on medium speed. Increase the speed medium-high and beat for 5 minutes, scraping down the bowl. Note that lumps may appear in the batter due to the temperature of the butter—this is fine.

SPOON or pipe the batter into the paper liners, filling them about two-thirds full. Lift up each pan and let it drop onto the countertop to burst any air bubbles and allow the batter to settle.

BAKE until the cupcakes spring back slightly when touched, and a toothpick inserted in the center of a cake comes out clean.

Yellow Cake Cupcakes

EQUIPMENT: 5- or 6-qt mixer

YIELD: 33 to 35 cupcakes

BAKING TIME: 12 to 15 minutes

12 oz (340 g) cake flour

1 Tbsp (16 g) baking powder

½ tsp (2.5 g) salt

8 oz (228 g) unsalted butter, softened

1 lb (454 g) granulated sugar

5 large eggs

2 tsp (10 ml) pure vanilla extract

10 oz (296 ml or 283 g) buttermilk

PREHEAT the oven to 350°F (177°C). Line cupcake pans with paper liners.

IN a medium bowl, sift together the flour, baking powder, and salt.

CUT up the butter into small pieces and place in the bowl of a stand mixer fitted with the paddle attachment. Beat on medium speed for 2 to 3 minutes until the butter is light and creamy in color.

ADD the sugar, ¼ cup at a time, beating 2 minutes after each addition. Scrape down the sides of the bowl occasionally. Add the eggs, one at a time, beating each in at 1-minute intervals.

REDUCE the speed to low. Stir the vanilla into the buttermilk. Add the dry ingredients alternately with the buttermilk mixture, beginning and ending with the dry ingredients. Mix just until incorporated. Scrape down the sides of the bowl and mix for 15 seconds more.

PIPE the batter into the paper liners, filling them about two-thirds full. Lift up each pan and let it drop onto the countertop to burst any air bubbles and allow the batter to settle.

CENTER the pans in the lower third of the oven and bake until a toothpick inserted in the center of a cake comes out clean.

Butter Cookies

EQUIPMENT: 5- or 6-qt mixer
YIELD: 3½ dozen cookies
BAKING TIME: 6 to 8 minutes

8 oz (228 g) unsalted butter

8 oz (228 g) granulated sugar

1 large egg

1 tsp (5 ml) pure vanilla extract

12 oz (340 g) all-purpose flour; plus extra for rolling out dough

1 tsp (3.5 g) baking powder

PREHEAT the oven to 350°F (177°C).

IN the bowl of a stand mixer fitted with the paddle attachment, cream the butter and sugar on medium speed for 2 minutes. Stop and scrape down the bowl, then cream the mixture for 1 minute more. Add the egg and vanilla extract and beat on medium speed until well combined.

SIFT together the flour and baking powder in a medium bowl. Add the flour mixture, 1 cup at a time, to the creamed butter and sugar mixture. Mix thoroughly on low to medium speed after each addition. Knead in the last cup of flour by hand. The dough will be stiff.

DIVIDE the dough into two balls. Wrap one ball in plastic wrap until ready to use. Divide the second ball of dough in half. On a floured surface, roll out one of the halves to a thickness of ⅛ to ¼ in. Run a large offset metal spatula under the dough as you roll to prevent it from sticking. Cut out cookies with cookie cutters, dipping the cutters into flour before each use.

CAREFULLY place the cut-out cookies onto ungreased nonstick cookie sheets or parchment paper–lined half-sheet pans. Bake until the edges of the cookies begin to brown lightly. Let the cookies cool on the cookie sheets until ready to use. Repeat with the remaining dough if making a full batch of cookies.

Lemon or Orange Cream Cookies

EQUIPMENT: 5- or 6-qt mixer

YIELD: 4 dozen cookies

BAKING TIME: 6 to 8 minutes

8 oz (228 g) unsalted butter

8 oz (228 g) granulated sugar

1 large egg

1 tsp (5 ml) lemon extract or orange extract

2 Tbsp (30 ml or 28.3 g) heavy cream

Grated zest of large lemon or medium orange

14 oz (397 g) all-purpose flour; plus extra for rolling out dough

1 tsp (3.5 g) baking powder

PREHEAT the oven to 350°F (177°C).

IN the bowl of a stand mixer fitted with the paddle attachment, cream the butter and sugar on medium speed for 2 minutes. Stop and scrape down the bowl, then cream the mixture for 1 minute more. Add the egg, lemon or orange extract, heavy cream, and lemon or orange zest to the creamed butter and sugar mixture and beat until well combined.

SIFT together the flour and baking powder in a medium bowl. Add the flour mixture, 1 cup at a time, to the creamed butter and sugar mixture. Mix thoroughly on low to medium speed after each addition. Knead in the last ½ cup of flour by hand. The dough will be stiff.

DIVIDE the dough into two balls. Wrap one ball in plastic wrap until ready to use. Divide the second ball of dough in half. On a floured surface, roll out one of the halves to a thickness of ⅛ to ¼ in. Run a large offset metal spatula under the dough as you roll it to prevent it from sticking. Cut out cookies with cookie cutters, dipping the cutters into flour before each use.

CAREFULLY place the cut-out cookies onto ungreased nonstick cookie sheets or parchment paper–lined half-sheet pans. Bake until the edges of the cookies begin to brown lightly. Let the cookies cool on the cookie sheets until ready to use. Repeat with the remaining dough if making a full batch of cookies.

Almond Paste Cookies

EQUIPMENT: 5- or 6-qt mixer
YIELD: 2½ dozen cookies
BAKING TIME: 6 to 8 minutes

6 oz (170 g) unsalted butter, softened

8 oz (228 g) granulated sugar

4 oz (114 g) almond paste

1 large whole egg

1 large egg yolk

1 tsp (5 ml) almond extract

10 oz (283 g) all-purpose flour, plus extra for rolling out dough

1 tsp (3.5 g) baking powder

½ tsp (2.5 g) salt

PREHEAT the oven to 350°F (177°C).

IN the bowl of a stand mixer fitted with the paddle attachment, cream the butter, sugar, and almond paste on medium speed for 2 minutes. Stop and scrape down the bowl, then cream the mixture for 1 minute more. Beat in the whole egg, the egg yolk, and the almond extract. Beat until the wet ingredients are absorbed and well combined.

SIFT together the flour, baking powder, and salt in a medium bowl. Add the flour mixture, 1 cup at a time, to the creamed butter and sugar mixture, mixing thoroughly on low to medium speed after each addition. Incorporate the last cup of flour by hand. The dough will be stiff.

DIVIDE the dough into two balls. Wrap one ball in plastic wrap until ready to use. On a floured surface, roll out the other ball to a thickness of ⅛ in. Run a large offset metal spatula under the dough as you roll to prevent it from sticking. Cut out cookies with cookie cutters, dipping the cutters into flour before each use.

CAREFULLY place the cut-out cookies onto ungreased nonstick cookie sheets or parchment paper–lined half-sheet pans. Bake until the edges of the cookies begin to brown lightly. Let the cookies cool on the cookie sheets until ready to use. Repeat with the remaining dough if making a full batch of cookies.

Chocolate Cookies

EQUIPMENT: 5- or 6-qt mixer

YIELD: 2½ to 3 dozen cookies

BAKING TIME: 6 to 8 minutes

8 oz (228 g) unsalted butter

5½ oz (156 g) granulated sugar

2½ oz (71 g) dark brown sugar, packed

1 large egg

1 Tbsp (15 ml) chocolate liqueur

12 oz (340 g) all-purpose flour; plus extra for rolling out dough

1¼ oz (35.4 g) Dutch-process cocoa powder

½ tsp (2 g) baking soda

¼ tsp (1.2 g) salt

PREHEAT the oven to 350°F (177°C).

IN the bowl of a stand mixer fitted with the paddle attachment, cream together the butter, granulated sugar, and brown sugar on medium speed for 2 minutes. Stop and scrape down the bowl, then cream the mixture for 30 to 60 seconds more. Beat in the egg and chocolate liqueur on medium speed until the wet ingredients are absorbed and well combined.

SIFT together the flour, cocoa powder, baking soda, and salt into a medium bowl. Add the flour mixture, 1 cup at a time, to the creamed mixture, mixing thoroughly on low to medium speed after each addition. Incorporate the last cup of flour by hand. The dough will be stiff.

DIVIDE the dough into two balls. Wrap one ball in plastic wrap until ready to use. On a floured surface, roll out the second ball to a thickness of ⅛ in. Run a large offset metal spatula under the dough as you roll to prevent it from sticking. Cut out cookies with cookie cutters, dipping the cutters into flour before each use.

CAREFULLY place the cut-out cookies onto ungreased nonstick cookie sheets or parchment paper–lined half-sheet pans. Bake until the edges of the cookies begin to brown lightly. Let the cookies cool on a cookie sheet until ready to use. Repeat with the remaining dough if making a full batch of cookies.

Pastillage

EQUIPMENT: 5- or 6-qt mixer

YIELD: 2 lb (908 g) paste

24 oz (680 g) confectioners' sugar

4 oz (114 g) cornstarch

3½ fl oz (104 ml or 99 g) cold water

1 tsp (2 g) cream of tartar

1 Tbsp (9 g) unflavored gelatin

1 tsp (3 g) Tylose CMC

SIFT the confectioners' sugar and cornstarch together into a medium bowl. Set aside.

IN a small microwave-safe bowl, combine the water and cream of tartar. Whisk with a wire whisk until dissolved. Slowly sprinkle in the gelatin and let it bloom. Microwave on high heat for 10 seconds. Whisk the mixture, then return it to the microwave and heat for another 10 seconds. Whisk again. Heat for a final 10 seconds and whisk until the gelatin and cream of tartar have dissolved.

PLACE the gelatin mixture in the bowl of a stand mixer fitted with the paddle attachment. On stir speed, add the confectioners' sugar and cornstarch mixture, a little at a time. When all of the dry ingredients have been mixed in, add the Tylose CMC and mix on medium speed for 2 minutes. Stop, scrape down the bowl, and beat the paste for 1 minute more. Remove the paste from the bowl and knead it together into a log. Wrap in plastic wrap and place the paste in an airtight container.

WHEN ready to use, break off a piece of the paste and knead with 1 to 2 Tbsp of cornstarch until pliable. Roll out on a small amount of cornstarch. Cut into the desired shapes.

THE pastillage paste will last for a few days in an airtight container at room temperature.

Lemon-Infused Buttercream Icing

EQUIPMENT: 5- or 6-qt mixer

YIELD: 2½ qt (2.4 L) icing

12 oz (355 mL) egg whites (10 large egg whites)

1½ lb (680 g) granulated sugar

Grated zest of 3 lemons

3 lb (1.36 kg) unsalted butter

3 oz (85 g) lemon curd

2 tsp (10 ml) lemon extract or 1 tsp (5 ml) lemon oil

LIGHTLY whisk the egg whites, sugar and lemon zest together in a bowl set over a saucepan of simmering water, or in a double boiler, until the mixture is hot to the touch and a candy thermometer reads 140°F (60°C). Strain the mixture immediately.

POUR the infused mixture into a room-temperature mixer bowl and whip, using the wire whisk attachment, on medium-high speed until doubled in volume. When you have finished mixing, the meringue should not move around in the bowl. Meanwhile, cut up the butter into medium-size pieces; the butter should be slightly moist on the outside but cold inside.

REPLACE the wire whisk with the paddle attachment. Divide the butter into four parts. Add the first part and mix on stir speed for 15 seconds. Then add the second part and mix on slow speed for 15 seconds, followed by the third and fourth parts. Slowly increase the speed of the mixer, starting on the lowest speed and increasing the speed every 10 seconds until you reach medium-high.

CONTINUE beating until the mixture begins to look light and fluffy. Stop the mixer and scrape down the bowl. Reduce the speed to low. Add the lemon curd and oil or extract and continue to beat on low speed for 45 seconds. Then beat on medium-high speed for 45 to 60 seconds.

STORE the buttercream in an airtight container for 1 week in the refrigerator or freeze for up to 3 months.

NOTE: *In hot weather, you can replace some of the butter with high-ratio shortening. High-ratio shortening is emulsified and contains water. It is not as greasy as commercial brands and does not leave an aftertaste on the back of your palate. High-ratio shortening can be substituted in any recipe that calls for butter or margarine. Popular brands are Sweetex and Alpine.*

For Orange-Infused Buttercream Icing, replace the lemon zest with orange zest and use orange curd instead of lemon curd and orange extract or oil instead of lemon extract or oil.

For Lime-Infused Buttercream Icing, add lime zest in place of lemon zest and lime curd instead of lemon curd, and lime extract or oil instead of lemon extract or oil.

Ganache

EQUIPMENT: 5- or 6-qt mixer

YIELD: 1¾ lb (794 g) ganache

12 fl oz (355 ml or 340 g) heavy cream

1 lb (454 g) semisweet, bittersweet, or white chocolate, chopped

IN a heavy-bottomed saucepan, bring the heavy cream to a boil. Turn off the heat. Add the chopped chocolate pieces or chocolate disks. Using a rubber spatula, stir the mixture until all the pieces of chocolate have melted.

POUR the chocolate mixture into a room-temperature bowl and cover with plastic wrap. If using semisweet or bittersweet chocolate, let the mixture stand at room temperature until the chocolate firms. If working with white chocolate, refrigerate the ganache until firm. White ganache will last for up to 2 weeks in the refrigerator. Dark ganache will last for several weeks in a cool dry kitchen.

Dark Chocolate Buttercream Icing

EQUIPMENT: 5- or 6-qt mixer

YIELD: 2½ to 3 qt (2.3 to 2.8l L) icing

1 lb (454 g) unsalted butter at room temperature

4 oz (115 g) white vegetable or high-ratio shortening

3 lb (1.36 kg) confectioners' sugar

4 oz (114 g) Dutch-process cocoa powder

3 Tbsp (24 g) meringue powder

1 tsp (5 g) salt

2 Tbsp (30 ml or 57 g) whole milk

1 Tbsp (15 ml) pure vanilla extract

5 fl oz (150 ml or 140 g) chocolate liqueur

1 lb (454 g) semisweet or bittersweet chocolate Ganache (page 186), left at room temperature to firm up

---

IN the bowl of a stand mixer fitted with the paddle attachment, cream the butter and shortening on medium speed for 2 minutes. Stop and scrape down the bowl, then cream the mixture for 1 minute more.

SIFT the confectioners' sugar and cocoa powder into a medium bowl. Add this mixture, 1 cup at a time, to the creamed butter and shortening and mix on low to medium speed until well blended. Add the meringue powder and salt and beat for 1 minute. The mixture will appear dry.

ADD the milk, vanilla, and chocolate liqueur to the buttercream. Beat on medium speed until well combined.

ADD the ganache, 1 cup at a time, and beat on medium speed until light and fluffy. When the icing is completed, keep the bowl covered with a damp cloth or plastic wrap to prevent the icing from drying. Store the icing in an airtight container for up to 2 weeks in the refrigerator, or freeze for up to 3 months.

Italian Meringue Buttercream

EQUIPMENT: 5- or 6-qt mixer

YIELD: 2¼ lb (1 kg) buttercream

1 lb (454 g) granulated sugar

8 fl oz (237 ml or 227 g) cold water

6 oz (177 ml) egg whites (6–7 large egg whites)

1 lb (454 g) unsalted butter, at room temperature

1 Tbsp (15 ml) pure vanilla extract

BRING the sugar and water to a boil in a medium pot. Wash down the insides of the pot with a pastry brush dipped in cold water to prevent crystallization of the sugar. When the sugar syrup comes to a boil, place a candy thermometer in the syrup.

WHEN the temperature reaches 215°F (102°C), in the bowl of the mixer fitted with the wire whisk, begin to whip the egg whites on high speed for 5 minutes, until they form stiff peaks. Meanwhile, check the sugar syrup.

WHEN the temperature reaches 238° to 240°F (114.5° to 116°C, soft-ball stage), remove the pot from the heat. Slowly pour the syrup in a steady stream down the inside of the mixer bowl while the whites are still whisking. Make sure the hot syrup doesn't touch the wire whisk.

CONTINUE whisking until the meringue is completely cool. This could take 6 to 10 minutes.

WITH the mixer still running, add the butter, a piece at a time, beating on low speed until all of the butter has been added. Add the vanilla and beat on medium-high speed until light and fluffy.

IF the buttercream gets too soft, refrigerate it for 15 to 20 minutes, then beat again until it begins to look light and fluffy. Store the buttercream in an air-tight container for 1 week in the refrigerator or freeze for up to 3 months.

Almond-Vanilla Buttercream Icing

EQUIPMENT: 5- or 6-qt mixer

YIELD: 1½ qt (1.41 L) icing

8oz (237 mL) egg whites (8–10 large egg whites)

1 lb (454 g) granulated sugar

1 lb (454 g) unsalted butter

8 oz (228 g) high-ratio shortening

1½ tsp (7.5 ml) pure vanilla extract

1½ tsp (7.5 ml) almond extract

LIGHTLY whisk the egg whites and sugar together in a bowl set over a saucepan of simmering water, or in a double boiler, until the mixture is hot to the touch and a candy thermometer reads 140°F (60°C).

POUR the hot whites into a room-temperature mixer bowl and whip with the wire whisk attachment on medium-high speed until doubled in volume. When you have finished mixing, the meringue should not move around in the bowl. Meanwhile, cut up the butter into medium pieces; the butter should be slightly moist on the outside but cold inside.

REPLACE the wire whisk with the paddle attachment. Divide the fat (butter and high-ratio shortening) into four parts. Add the first part and mix on stir speed for 15 seconds. Then add the second part and mix on slow speed for 15 seconds, followed by the third and fourth parts. Slowly increase the speed of the mixer, starting on the lowest speed and raising the speed every 10 seconds until you reach medium-high.

CONTINUE beating until the mixture begins to look light and fluffy. Stop the mixer and scrape down the bowl. Reduce the speed to low. Add the vanilla and almond extracts and continue to beat on low speed for 45 seconds. Then beat on medium-high speed for 45 to 60 seconds.

STORE the buttercream in an airtight container for 1 week in the refrigerator or freeze for up to 3 months.

Coconut-Rum Buttercream Icing

EQUIPMENT: 5- or 6-qt mixer

YIELD: 5 lb (2.3 kg) icing

1 lb (454 g) unsalted butter

8 oz (230 g) white vegetable or high-ratio shortening

2 Tbsp (30 ml or 28 g) coconut extract or oil

1 tsp (5 g) salt

3 lb (1.36 kg) confectioners' sugar

3 Tbsp (24 g) meringue powder

3 fl oz (89 ml or 85 g) coconut milk

1 fl oz (30 ml or 28 g) coconut rum or light rum

IN the bowl of a stand mixer fitted with the paddle attachment, cream the butter and shortening on medium-high speed for 3 minutes. Stop and scrape down the bowl, then cream for 1 minute more. Add the coconut oil or extract and the salt and mix until combined. Gradually add the sugar, and then the meringue powder. The mixture will appear dry.

ADD the coconut milk and rum and beat on medium-high speed until light and fluffy, 5 to 8 minutes. When the icing is completed, keep the bowl covered with a damp cloth or plastic wrap to prevent the icing from drying.

STORE the icing in an airtight container for 2 weeks in the refrigerator or freeze for up to 3 months.

Decorator's Buttercream Icing

EQUIPMENT: 5- or 6-qt mixer
YIELD: 5 lb (2.3 kg) icing

1 lb (454 g) unsalted butter

8 oz (230 g) white vegetable or high-ratio shortening

1½ tsp (7.5 ml) lemon, vanilla, or almond extract

1 tsp (5 g) salt

3 lb (1.36 kg) confectioners' sugar

3 Tbsp (24 g) meringue powder

4½ fl oz (134 ml or 128 g) water, whole milk, heavy cream, or clear liqueur

---

IN the bowl of a stand mixer fitted with the paddle attachment, cream the butter and shortening on medium-high speed for 3 minutes. Stop and scrape down the bowl, then cream for 1 minute more. Add the lemon, vanilla, or almond extract and the salt and mix until combined. Gradually add the sugar, and then the meringue powder. The mixture will appear dry.

ADD the liquid of your choice and beat on medium-high speed until light and fluffy, 5 to 8 minutes. Once the icing is completed, keep the bowl covered with a damp cloth or plastic wrap to prevent the icing from drying.

STORE the icing in an airtight container for 2 weeks in the refrigerator or freeze for up to 3 months.

French Vanilla Buttercream

EQUIPMENT: 5- or 6-qt mixer

YIELD: 2½ to 3 lb (1.1 to 1.4 kg) buttercream

12 oz (340 g) granulated sugar

6 fl oz (177 ml or 170 g) whole milk

1 Tbsp plus 1½ tsp (⅜ oz or 10.6 g) all-purpose flour

¼ tsp (1.25 g) salt

1 Tbsp (15 ml) pure vanilla extract

1¼ lb (568 g) unsalted butter, cut into small pieces

3 fl oz (89 ml or 85 g) heavy cream

MAKE a custard by heating the sugar and milk in a bowl set over a saucepan of simmering water, or in a double boiler, until the sugar crystals dissolve. Remove from the heat, add the flour, salt, and vanilla and whisk until the flour is incorporated. Place over an ice bath until the custard has cooled slightly.

POUR the custard mixture into the bowl of a mixer fitted with the paddle attachment. Add the cut-up butter and heavy cream and mix on low speed until the ingredients are fully incorporated and until the mixture starts to thicken.

MIX on the next highest speed until the mixture starts to look light and fluffy. This can take 7 to 10 minutes or even longer if making larger batches.

STORE the buttercream in an airtight container for 2 weeks in the refrigerator or freeze for up to 3 months.

NOTE: *If the buttercream curdles, it will just take a longer time for the butter to warm up. Continue beating until the butter softens and the mixture looks light and fluffy.*

Swiss Meringue Buttercream

EQUIPMENT: 5- or 6-qt mixer

YIELD: 2½ qt (2.4 L) buttercream

12 oz (355 mL) egg whites (10–12 large egg whites)

1½ lb (680 g) granulated sugar

3 lb (1.36 kg) unsalted butter

2 Tbsp (30 ml) lemon, almond, vanilla, or orange extract, or up to 3 fl oz (89 ml or 85 g) light rum, framboise, kirsch, amaretto, or poire William

LIGHTLY whisk the egg whites and sugar together in a double boiler or in a bowl set over a saucepan of simmering water until the mixture is hot to the touch and a candy thermometer reads 140°F (60°C).

POUR the hot whites into a room-temperature mixer bowl and whip using the wire whisk attachment on medium-high speed until doubled in volume. When you have finished mixing, the meringue should not move around in the bowl. Meanwhile, cut up the butter into medium pieces; the butter should be slightly moist on the outside but cold inside.

REPLACE the wire whisk with the paddle attachment. Divide the butter into four parts. Add the first part and mix on stir speed for 15 seconds. Then add the second part and mix on slow speed for 15 seconds, followed by the third and fourth parts. Slowly increase the speed of the mixer, starting on the lowest speed and raising the speed every 10 seconds until you reach medium-high.

CONTINUE beating until the mixture begins to look light and fluffy. Stop the mixer and scrape down the bowl. Reduce the speed to low. Add the flavoring and continue to beat on low speed for 45 seconds. Then increase the speed and beat on medium-high speed for 45 to 60 seconds.

STORE the buttercream in an airtight container for 1 week in the refrigerator or freeze for up to 3 months.

NOTE: *In hot weather, you can replace some of the butter with high-ratio shortening. High-ratio shortening is emulsified and contains water. It is not as greasy as commercial brands and does not leave an aftertaste on the back of your palate. High-ratio shortening can be substituted in any recipe that calls for butter or margarine. Popular brands are Sweetex and Alpine.*

Confectioners' Glaze (Gum Glue)

YIELD: 6 oz (170 g) glaze

6 fl oz (177 ml or 170 g) water

2 Tbsp (24 g) gum arabic

Small bottle with lid

COMBINE the water and gum arabic in a small bottle with a lid. Shake vigorously for 30 seconds. Let the formula sit for 30 minutes and then shake vigorously again.

STORE in the refrigerator. (The glaze will develop a sour smell if left at room temperature for more than 1 day.)

NOTE: *Use this glaze on showpieces that require a high sheen.*

Marzipan

EQUIPMENT: 5- or 6-qt mixer
YIELD: 2 lb (907 g) marzipan

1 lb (454 g) almond paste

1 lb (454 g) confectioners' sugar, plus a little more if needed

1 tsp (5 ml) pure vanilla extract

1 tsp (5 ml) light rum

3 fl oz (89 ml or 126 g) light corn syrup

CUT up the almond paste with a bench scraper and place in the bowl of the stand mixer fitted with the paddle attachment. Mix on low speed until some of the oil is extracted from the paste, about 30 seconds.

ADD ½ lb (227 g) of the sugar and continue to mix while slowly pouring in the vanilla, rum, and corn syrup. Mix on low to medium speed until the dough comes together and sticks to the paddle. Remove the paste from the paddle.

SIFT the remaining sugar onto the countertop. Turn the dough out onto the sugar and knead in all of the sugar. If the dough is still sticky, knead in a little extra sugar. Knead until the marzipan has a fine, smooth texture. The mixture should feel soft but firm.

DOUBLE-WRAP the marzipan in plastic wrap and store in the refrigerator until ready to use. The marzipan will keep in the refrigerator for several months.

NOTE: *Corn syrup and molasses are heavier than thinner liquids like water, milk, and juice. Instead of measuring roughly the same number of ounces in volume and weight, the weight will be 1½ times the volume. Thus, 3 fl oz (89 ml) of corn syrup will weigh not 3 oz (85 g) but 4½ oz (126 g).*

Modeling Chocolate (Chocolate Plastic)

YIELD: Approximately 1½ lb (680 g) modeling paste

DARK MODELING CHOCOLATE

1 lb (454 g) semisweet, bittersweet, or milk chocolate

5 fl oz (148 ml or 210 g) light corn syrup

WHITE MODELING CHOCOLATE

1 lb (454 g) white chocolate

4 fl oz (118 ml or 168 g) corn syrup

FINELY chop the chocolate and place it in a bowl set over a saucepan of simmering water. Stir to melt the chocolate evenly. Remove the bowl from the saucepan when the chocolate is three-quarters melted and continue to stir until all the pieces have melted. Add the corn syrup all at once, and using a rubber spatula, stir until the chocolate starts to leave the sides of the bowl. For dark chocolate, this process will take about 1 minute. For white or milk chocolate, the process will take 20 to 30 seconds.

SCRAPE the chocolate mixture onto a piece of plastic wrap. Spread out the chocolate to a thickness ¼ to ½ in (6 mm to 1.3 cm). Place another piece of plastic wrap on top of the chocolate. Refrigerate or set aside in a cool, dry place to age for 24 hours.

ONCE aged, cut the chocolate plastic into smaller pieces and microwave the pieces for a few seconds just to take the hard edge off the chocolate. Knead thoroughly with the heel of your hands until the chocolate has elasticity and a shiny coat. Wrap in plastic wrap until ready to use. The chocolate plastic will last for several weeks in a cool dry room.

White Modeling Chocolate Paste

YIELD: 1¼ lb (567 g) modeling paste

1 lb (454 g) white chocolate

4 fl oz (118 ml or 168 g) light corn syrup

Commercial rolled fondant (optional, see note)

Newsprint paper

Cornstarch

MELT the chocolate in a bowl set over a saucepan of simmering water until two-thirds melted. Remove the bowl from the saucepan and stir until all of the pieces have melted.

POUR in the corn syrup all at once and immediately begin to stir the corn syrup with a rubber spatula. Continue to stir for about 30 seconds, until the chocolate thickens and looks slightly grainy. Do not overstir or you will ruin the chocolate.

SPREAD the chocolate out on a piece of newsprint paper. The chocolate should be about ⅛ in (3 mm) thick. Place in the refrigerator until firm, 2 to 4 hours.

REMOVE the chocolate from the paper, wrap the chocolate in plastic wrap, and refrigerate for 24 hours to complete the aging process. The next day, knead the chocolate with a little cornstarch until the chocolate is pliable.

NOTES: *To color white chocolate, you must use oil-based colors. If you wish to use water-based colors, then you must add some commercial rolled fondant to the chocolate to temper the chocolate. In addition, if you wish the white chocolate to be more elastic or more manageable, adding the commercial rolled fondant will give you that.*

First, weigh the chocolate. Add 2 parts white chocolate to 1 part commercial rolled fondant. Knead in as much cornstarch as needed to absorb the fat. Second, color the chocolate as desired and then wrap in plastic wrap and refrigerate for several hours before use. Otherwise, the chocolate will be much too soft to use.

Corn syrup and molasses are heavier than thinner liquids like water, milk, and juice. Instead of measuring roughly the same number of ounces in volume and weight, the weight will be 1½ times the volume. Thus, 4 fl oz (118 ml) of corn syrup will weigh not 4 oz (114 g) but 6 oz (168 g).

Newsprint paper is inexpensive paper that shoes and glassware are often packed with to absorb moisture. You can purchase this paper at any art supply store.

Egg White Royal Icing

EQUIPMENT: 5- or 6-qt mixer

YIELD: 1 lb (454 g) icing

3 oz (89 ml) egg whites (3–4 large egg whites) or pasteurized egg whites, at room temperature

1 lb (454 g) confectioners' sugar, sifted

½ tsp (2.5 ml) lemon extract

IN the bowl of the stand mixer fitted with the paddle attachment, lightly whip the egg whites on medium speed until the whites are frothy and form soft peaks. This will take about 3 minutes. Lower the speed and gradually add the sugar. Add the lemon extract and beat on medium-high speed for 5 to 8 minutes, or until the icing forms medium to stiff peaks. Cover the icing with plastic wrap and store for up to 1 day in a glass container until ready to use.

Meringue Powder Royal Icing

EQUIPMENT: 5- or 6-qt mixer

YIELD: 1¼ lb (571 g) icing

1⅜ oz (40 g) meringue powder

4 fl oz (118 ml or 114 g) cold water

1 lb (454 g) confectioners' sugar, sifted

½ tsp (2.5 ml) lemon extract

COMBINE the meringue powder and the cold water in the bowl of the stand mixer fitted with the paddle attachment. Beat on medium-high speed to soft peaks, about 3 minutes. Slowly add the sugar.

ADD the lemon extract and beat for 5 minutes on medium-high speed, or until the icing forms medium to stiff peaks. Cover the icing with plastic wrap until ready to use.

THE icing need not be refrigerated if kept in a cool dry place and used within 2 weeks. Beat again before using.

Quick Gumpaste

YIELD: 1 lb (454 g) gumpaste

1 lb (454 g) commercial rolled fondant

1 tsp (5 ml or 3 g) Tylose CMC

½ tsp (2.5 ml) white vegetable shortening

KNEAD the fondant until pliable. If the fondant is sticky, knead in a little cornstarch to prevent sticking.

NEXT, make a well in the center of the rolled fondant. Add the Tylose.

RUB the shortening into your palms and knead the paste for 3 to 5 minutes. Double-wrap the paste in plastic wrap and place in a zipper-lock plastic bag or an airtight container. Let rest in the refrigerator (or a cool, dry place) until ready to use. This paste can be used immediately but will perform better if allowed to rest for 24 hours. The gumpaste will last for months stored in the refrigerator.

NOTE: *Tylose can be replaced with 1½ to 2 tsp (7.5 to 10 ml) gum tragacanth, but the paste will need to rest for 12 to 24 hours before use.*

Flood Icing

YIELD: 9 oz (255 g) icing

½ to 1 oz (15 to 30 ml or 14 to 28 g) water or pasteurized egg whites

8 oz (227 g) Egg White Royal Icing or Meringue Powder Royal Icing (page 198 or 199)

CAREFULLY stir the water or egg whites into the royal icing, a little at a time. After adding half the liquid, check to see if you have reached the proper consistency. Continue to add the liquid until you have achieved a flow consistency. Add more liquid if necessary. Cover with plastic wrap to prevent drying. Store the icing in an airtight container for up to 3 days in the refrigerator.

HOW TO CHECK FOR FLOW CONSISTENCY

YOU have achieved a flow consistency if, after you draw a knife through the icing, the icing completely comes back together after you count to 10 seconds. If the icing comes together before 7 seconds, add a little more royal icing to thicken it. Check for consistency again. If the icing does not come together within 10 seconds, add a little more liquid.

Lemon, Lime, or Orange Curd

YIELD: 2½ lb (1.1 kg) curd

8 large eggs (approximately 14 oz)

2 egg yolks (approximately 1 oz)

1½ lb (680 g) granulated sugar

Grated zest of 10 lemons, limes, or medium oranges

Juice of 10 lemons, limes, or medium oranges (12 fl oz/355 ml or 340 g)

12 oz (340 g) unsalted butter, cut into ½-in (1.3 cm) pieces

USING a whisk, beat the whole eggs, egg yolks, and sugar together in a stainless steel bowl until well combined. Add the zest, juice, and butter.

COOK in a bowl set over a saucepan of simmering water, or in a double boiler, stirring constantly, until the curd starts to thicken, about 20 minutes. The curd is ready when it coats the back of a spoon. Strain immediately and cool over an ice bath.

STORE the curd in a plastic container with plastic wrap placed directly on the surface to prevent a skin from forming. Then cover with a tight-fitting lid. Refrigerate until ready to use. The curd will last for 2 weeks in the refrigerator.

NOTE: *More lemons, limes, or oranges may be needed to equal 12 fl oz (355 ml or 340 g). You could also use unsweetened orange juice instead of squeezing the juice from the fresh orange.*

Sieved Apricot Jam

YIELD: 10 oz (283 g) jam

8 oz (227 g) apricot preserves

4 fl oz (118 ml) cold water

IN a saucepan, combine the preserves and water and bring to a simmer. Strain and allow the mixture to cool. Place the jam in a jar with a tight-fitting lid. Refrigerate until ready to use.

APPENDIX OF PATTERNS

This selection of patterns can be used to reproduce the cake designs shown in this book. Some of the patterns can be enlarged or reduced to fit your own designs. All of the patterns are shown sized to 100% of the original design unless otherwise noted.

Brush Embroidery Pattern

(Pattern shown at smaller size for fit. Enlarge to 119%.)

Nirvana Cake Patterns

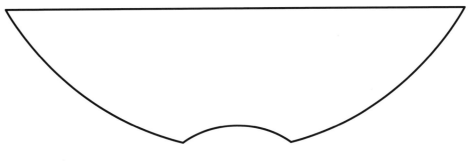

Top Overlay A

Bottom Overlay

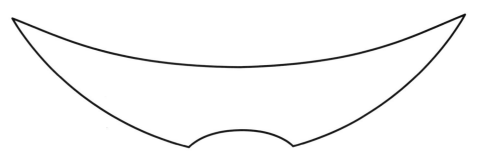

Bottom Panel B

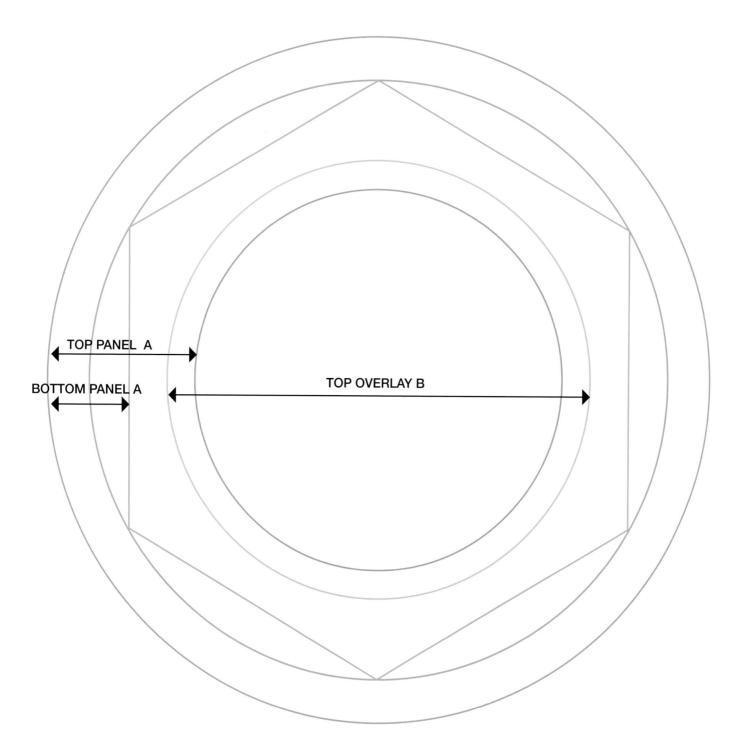

Top Panel A, Bottom Panel A, and Top Overlay B

(Pattern shown at smaller size for fit. Enlarge to 164%.)

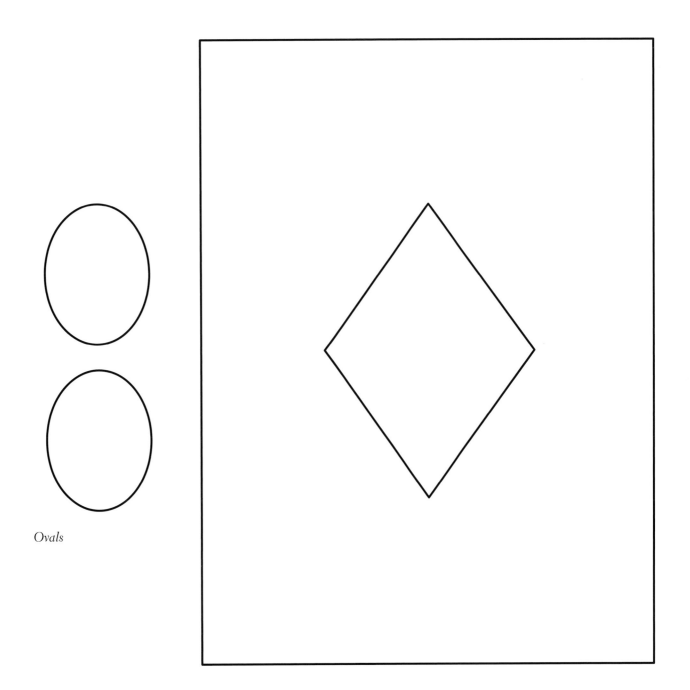

Ovals

Side Panel

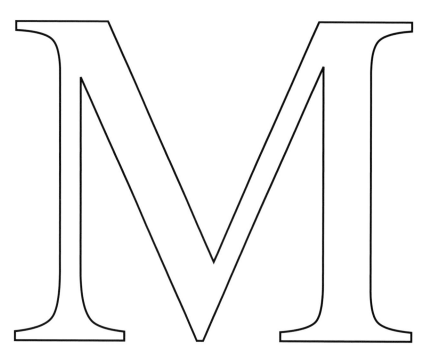

Monogram

Pansy Spray

Venetian Mask

(Pattern shown at smaller size for fit.
Enlarge to 119%.)

209

Antique Clock Patterns

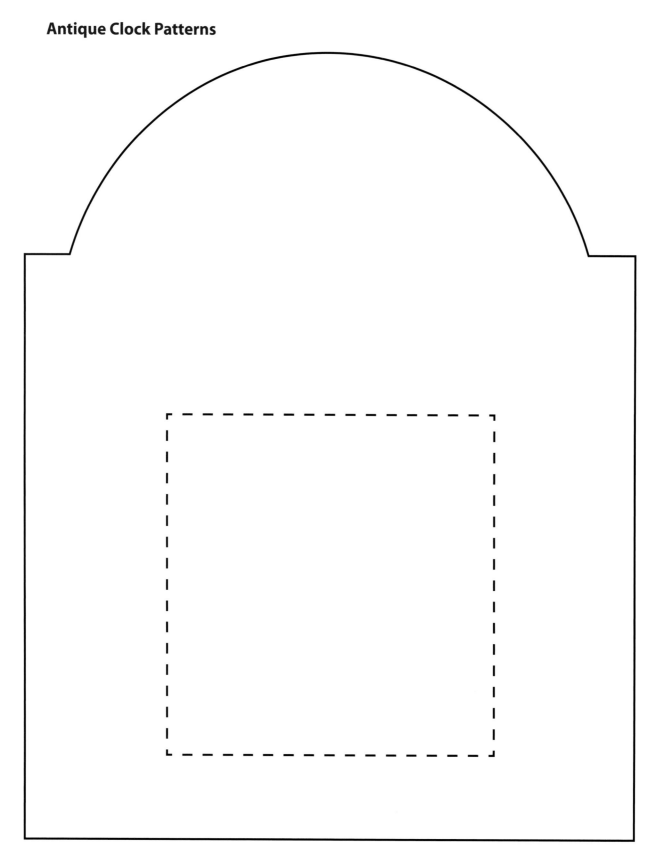

Panel A, Front of Clock

Panel B, Back of Clock

Panel D, E, F, Side and Bottom of Clock

Panel C, Arch

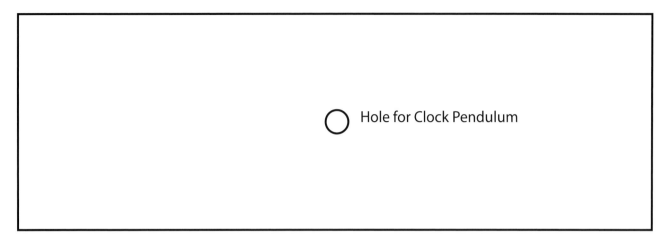

Panel G, Panel Under the Arch

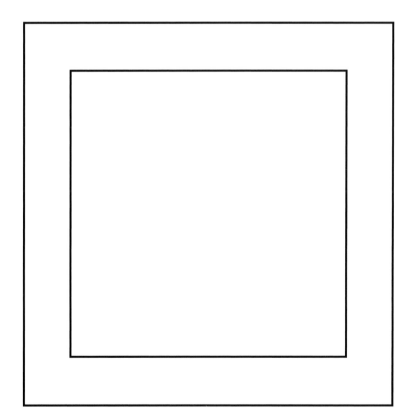

Clock Door

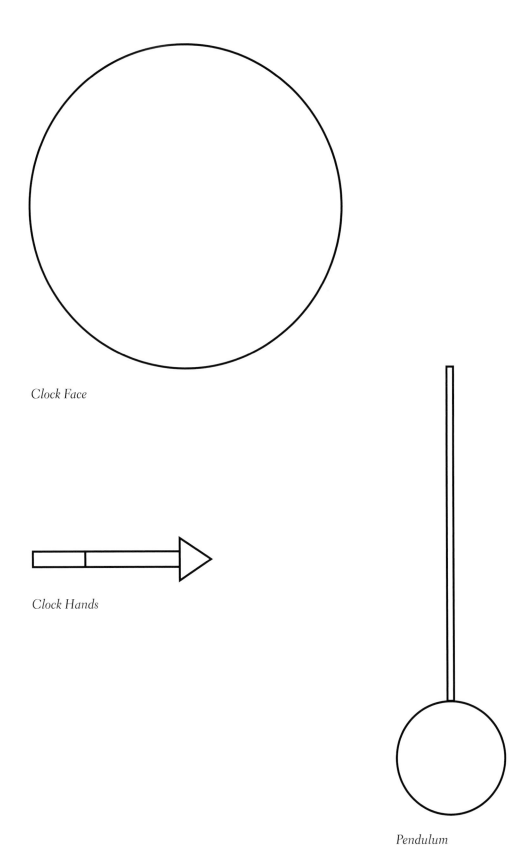

Clock Face

Clock Hands

Pendulum

Crescents and Scroll Cake Patterns

Monogram

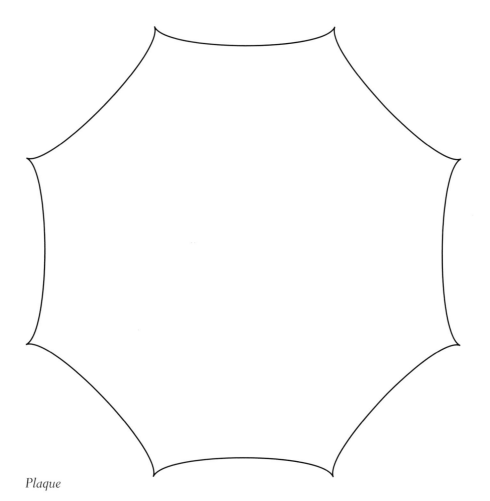

Plaque

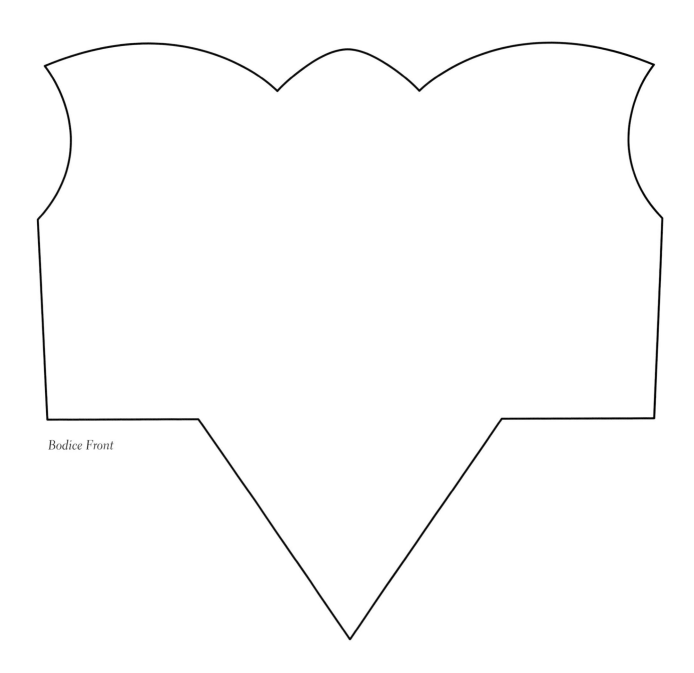

Bodice Front

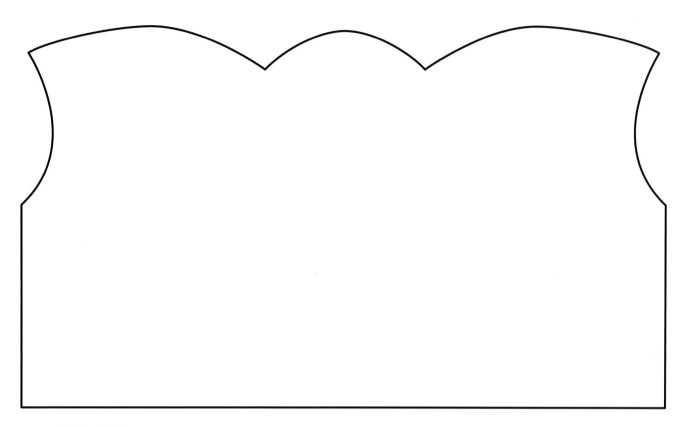

Bodice Back

Dress Panel

Bountiful! Cake Patterns

Pumpkin Leaf

Pumpkin Panel

INDEX

A

African daisy, gumpaste, 42, 44, 46–47
airbrushing, 94, 102, 134, 135, 137
allergies, 5
Almond Paste Cookies, 181
Almond Paste Cupcakes, 176
Almond-Vanilla Buttercream Icing, 189
anniversary cakes, 34–55
Antique Clock, 96–103, 210–214
appendix of patterns, 204–219
apple, marzipan, 161, 162
apple blossom, royal icing, 22–23
Apricot Jam, Sieved, 203
artist tray, 28, 31, 76
Australian Stringwork Cake, 50–55
Australian style, 9, 151
autumn. *See* fall designs

B

baking skills, 4
bamboo, gumpaste, 90, 92–95
Bamboo Cake, 90–95
Banana-Rum Cake, 175
Basket-weave Cupcake, 158, 159
bells, gumpaste, 128–129
berries
    gumpaste, 36, 41, 126, 131
    marzipan, 160–161
birthday cakes, 56–81
blossoms. *See* flowers; *specific blossom types*
board. *See* cake board
borders
    bead (oval), 52
    piped rope, 88
    ribbon, 140, 152
bottle, squeeze, 17, 18
Bountiful!, 132–139, 219

bows
    fabric ribbon, 55
    gumpaste ribbon, 74, 80–81
Brush Embroidery Cake, 36–41, 204
brush embroidery technique, 15–16, 38–39
brushes
    pastry, 11, 79, 80
    sable, 16, 28, 52, 76, 99, 101, 142
buds, gumpaste, 28, 49, 140, 145
Butter Cookies, 179
buttercream. *See under* recipes, icing
butterflies, flood icing, 17–18

C

cake board
    fondant-covered, 36, 85, 140
    panel construction on, 69, 70, 72
cakes
    anniversary, 34–55
    birthday, 56–81
    circumference, measuring technique, 52, 79, 108, 122
    examples (*See* design examples, cakes)
    groom's, 82–103
    marking technique, 52
    recipes, 166–175
    seasonal, 124–147
    shape
        dome, 59
        spherical, 42, 132
        triangle, 85
    sturdiness, 121
    wedding, 104–123
calligraphy, achieving mastery, 3
cameo, gumpaste, 74, 80–81
carbon copy method, 15, 76, 111

cell pad, construction base
  calyx, 137
  leaves, 29, 41, 136
  petals, 48, 61
  plunger flowers, 11
cheese grater, 160, 161
cherry blossoms
  gumpaste, 140, 144–146
  royal icing, 22–23
chincherinchee (Star of Bethlehem), gumpaste,
    48–49
chocolate. *See also under* recipes
  ganache, 153, 186
  modeling or plastic (*See* modeling chocolate)
  sprayed-on, 85, 87
Chocolate Cookies, 182
Chocolate Fudge Cupcakes, 177
circumference of cake, measuring technique, 52, 79,
    108, 122
classes, 2, 4
clay gun, 14, 15, 93, 115, 119, 163
Clock, Antique, 96–103, 210–214
cloves, 161, 162, 163
cocoa butter, 87
Coconut-Rum Buttercream Icing, 190
colors, mixing, 76. *See also* food color
Confectioners' Glaze (Gum Glue), 194
cookies
  examples (*See* design examples, cookies)
  inspiration, 151
  popularity and trends, 149
  recipes, 179–182
corn, gumpaste, 132, 137, 139
cornelli lace, 8, 50, 54
cornmeal, 44
corn syrup, 153, 154, 161, 163, 195
cotton
  to prop gumpaste decorations, 61, 62, 80, 87
  thread, for stamens, 144, 145
Courtly Dress, 112–119, 216–218
Cream Cheese Pound Cake, 174
Crescents and Scroll Cake, 106–111, 215
Cricut, 3

cupcakes
  examples (*See* design examples, cupcakes)
  inspiration, 157
  popularity and trends, 149
  recipes, 176–178
Cupcake with Marzipan Fruit, 161–163
Cupcake with Marzipan Raspberries, 160–161
Cupcake with Piped Rosettes, 158, 159
Cupcake with Sweet Pea Clusters, 156, 158–160
curd, recipe, 202
cutters
  cookie, 52, 153
  daisy, 118
  fluted, 101
  leaf, 29, 40, 131, 136
  oval petal, 44
  plunger, 10–11
  rose calyx, 40, 61, 72, 95, 118, 136
  round tip as, 116
cutting machine, electric. *See* Cricut
cylinder, gumpaste, 92–93

D

Dark Chocolate Buttercream Icing, 187
Dark Modeling Chocolate, 196
Decorator's Buttercream Icing, 191
design. *See also* inspiration
  modified from another format, 151
  modified from another's original concept, 1, 5, 37
  process, 2–3
  software, 2
design examples. *See also* patterns; transfer
    techniques
  cakes
    Antique Clock, 96–103, 210–214
    Australian Stringwork Cake, 50–55
    Bamboo Cake, 90–95
    Bountiful!, 132–139, 219
    Brush Embroidery Cake, 36–41, 204
    Courtly Dress, 112–119, 216–218
    Crescents and Scroll Cake, 106–111, 215
    Headdress Cake, 42–49

design examples *(continued)*
    Ms. Constance's Hat, 58–65
    Nirvana Cake, 66–73, 205–208
    Oriental Stringwork Cake, 120–123
    Season's Greetings, 126–131
    Spring Love, 140–147
    Tiffany-Inspired Ribbon Cake, 74–81, 208
    Venetian Mask Cake, 84–89, 209
  cookies
    Dome Cookie, 152–153
    Round Chocolate Fan Cookie and Upright
      Heart-Shaped Cookie, 154–155
    Textured Iced Cookie, 155
  cupcakes
    Basket-weave Cupcake, 158, 159
    Cupcake with Marzipan Fruit, 161–163
    Cupcake with Marzipan Raspberries,
      160–161
    Cupcake with Piped Rosettes, 158, 159
    Cupcake with Sweet Pea Clusters, 156, 158–
      160
Devil's Food Cake, 170
dietary needs, special, 5
dogbone tool
  to shape petal, 48
  to soften calyx, 136
  to soften leaf, 29, 41, 64, 136
  to soften petal, 10, 11
Dome Cookie, 152–153
dowel, to shape decorations
  bamboo stalk, 92–93
  pea pod, 138
  spiral foliage, 30, 31
drapery, gumpaste or fondant
  classical, 12–13
  freehand, 11–12, 42, 44–45, 85, 89
  pleated, 112, 114–115, 119
drop strings (trellis piping)
  Australian stringwork, 50, 53, 54
  Oriental stringwork, 120–123
  with scrollwork, 108
drying times
  flood icing
    butterfly, 17, 18

    monogram, 71
    panel, 69, 70, 101
  fondant dome, 153
  gel food color, painting, 79
  gumpaste
    bamboo, 92
    bell, 129
    berry, 41
    bow, 80
    bud, 28
    cameo, 80
    flower, 27, 44
    leaf, 41, 64, 136
    mask, 87
    pea pod, 138
  modeling chocolate rope, 163
  royal icing
    drop string, 108, 123
    marker, 122
    scrollwork, 108
  sprayed-on chocolate, 87
dusting. *See* petal dusting

E

egg white
  in brush embroidery technique, 15, 16, 39
  to thin icing, 17, 21
Egg White Royal Icing, 198
embossing, 65, 116, 137, 155. *See also* molds and
    presses
embroidery techniques
  brush
    examples, 38–39
    technique, 15–16
  freehand piping
    examples, 39, 79, 100, 152, 154
    technique, 9–10
English style. *See* Nirvana Cake; Nirvana style; Simnel
    Cake
extension work. *See* piping, stringwork

F

fall designs, 25, 31, 132–139
five-petal flowers, royal icing, 22–23, 55
Flood Icing, 201
flooding (runout)
　examples
　　butterfly, 17–18
　　clock hands, 100
　　monogram, 71
　　panels, see-through, 66, 68–70, 73
　technique, 17–18
florets, 11, 27, 144
flowers. *See also* leaves; *specific flower types*
　brush embroidery, tulips, 36, 37–38
　gumpaste
　　African daisy, 42, 44, 46–47
　　blossoms, 26–27
　　blossoms, cherry, 140, 144–146
　　buds, 28, 140, 145
　　calyx, 61, 72, 118, 136
　　chincherinchee, 48–49
　　floral arrangement skills used in, 4
　　gardenia, 58, 60–62
　　plunger flowers (*See* plunger flowers)
　icing, 21–24
　　calyx, 24
　　five-petal blossoms, basic, 22–23, 55
　　sepals, 24
　　stamens, 23, 24
　　sweet peas, 24, 158–160
　　violets, 23–24
　medallion, 112, 118–119
　painted
　　forget-me-nots, 142, 143
　　pansies, 74, 76–79, 208
　　stamens, 79
　stamens, 23, 24, 79, 144, 145
flute, 158, 160
foliage. *See also* leaves
　gumpaste, 29–31
　wire spiral, 30, 31, 95
fondant
　achieving mastery, 4
　rolled
　　chocolate, 85
　　covering a cake, 50, 126, 140
　　covering cake board, 85, 140
　　draped, 11–12, 42, 44–45, 85, 89
　　molded dome, 152, 153
　　strips over a sphere, 132, 134
　　tassels, 14
　　textured, 58, 63, 65
food color
　gel, 76–79, 142–143
　mixing technique, 76
　shadow and highlight technique, 76, 79
forget-me-nots
　painted, 142, 143
　royal icing, 22, 23
French Vanilla Buttercream, 192
fruit, marzipan, 160–163

G

ganache
　as cookie filling, 153
　piped rosettes, 26
　recipe, 186
gilding
　clock, 88, 98, 99, 100, 103
　mask, 88
　medallion, 118, 119
glaze, recipe, 194
gold powder. *See* gilding
grater, 160, 161
groom's cakes, 82–103
Gum Glue, 194
gumpaste
　achieving mastery, 4
　recipe, 200
　steam to create shine, 31, 41, 64
gun. *See* clay gun; Wagner Spray gun

H

Headdress Cake, 42–49
heart, wire spiral, 140, 146–147
heart-shaped cookie, 154–155

I

icing
  flood, 52, 201 (*See also* flooding)
  marzipan as, 67
  modeling chocolate as, 154, 155
  to outline a flooded area, 17, 18, 100
  recipes, 184–193, 198–199, 201
  royal
    egg white to thin, 17, 21
    markers, 122
    as piping (*See* piping)
    recipes, 198–199
icing nail, 22, 23, 24
initials. *See* monograms
inspiration
  architecture, 1, 67
  from books and magazines, 2
  fashion and costume, 1, 43, 59, 85, 113
  movies, 43
  plants, 91, 127, 133
  seasons, 127, 133, 141
  specific objects, 75, 96
  from travel, 85, 91
Italian Meringue Buttercream, 188

K

Kleinman, Cheryl, 151
knife. *See* X-acto knife

L

lace
  piped, cornelli, 8, 50, 54
  texture, 155

Lambeth, Joseph, 1, 107
lattice, 19, 99
leaves
  gumpaste
    corn, 137, 139
    cutter for, 29–31, 40–41, 72, 95, 126, 131
    gardenia, 58, 64
    maple, 132, 136
    pumpkin, 132, 136–137
    textured (*See* molds and presses, leaf)
  painted, 76–79, 140, 142–143
  piped, 25, 39, 158, 159, 161, 163
Lemon Cream Pound Cake, 168
Lemon Curd, 202
Lemon-Infused Buttercream Icing, 184–185
Lemon or Orange Cream Cookies, 180
letters. *See* monograms
Lime Curd, 202
Lime-Infused Buttercream Icing, 185

M

marker, 122, 123
marzipan
  corn syrup to create shine, 161, 163
  fruit, 160–163
  as icing, 67
  recipe, 195
marzipan tool, serrated, 160, 161
mask, Venetian, 84–89, 209
mastery, achieving, 3–4
medallion, gumpaste, 112, 118–119
Meringue Powder Royal Icing, 199
Microsoft Word, 2
modeling chocolate
  in cookies, 153, 154–155
  recipes, 196–197
  rope, 162, 163
modeling paste
  drapery, 11–12
  recipe, 197
modeling stick, 26–27, 64, 144
molds and presses

bell, 128
cameo, 80
fan, 154
half-sphere, 153
lace-textured, 155
leaf, 29, 41, 136, 137
mask, 87
monograms
  for anniversary cakes, 35
  flooded, 71
  patterns, 208, 215
  piped onto plaque, 111
Ms. Constance's Hat, 58–65

N

nail, icing, 22, 23, 24
Nirvana Cake, 66–73, 205–208
Nirvana style, 1, 67

O

orange, marzipan, 161–163
orange blossom, royal icing, 22–23
Orange Cream Cookies, 180
Orange Cream Pound Cake, 167
Orange Curd, 202
Orange-Infused Buttercream Icing, 185
Oriental Stringwork Cake, 120–123
overpiping. See piping, overpiping

P

painting techniques
  airbrush, 94, 102, 134, 135, 137
  brush embroidery, 15–16, 38–39
  brushing with gel food colors, 76–79, 140, 142–
    143
  chocolate spray, 85, 87
  gold powder (See gilding)
panels. See also plaques

brocade-like, 112, 116, 117
clock, 98
make extra in case of breakage, 69
see-through, 66, 68–70, 73
pansies, painted, 74, 76–79, 208
paper
  adding machine, 52, 79, 108, 122
  parchment, 21, 22, 23, 24, 86, 116
  see-through, 9, 15, 38
Pastillage, 183
pastry skills, 4
patterns, 204–219. See also transfer techniques
  Antique Clock, 210–214
  Bountiful!, 219
  Brush Embroidery Cake, 204
  Courtly Dress, 216–218
  Crescents and Scroll Cake, 215
  monograms, 208, 215
  Nirvana Cake, 205–208
  Tiffany-Inspired Ribbon Cake, 208
  Venetian Mask Cake, 209
peach blossom, royal icing, 22–23
pear, marzipan, 161, 162
pearl luster, 74, 79
peas in a pod, gumpaste, 132, 138–139
pencil, 2
petal dusting
  buds, 28
  cones, flower, 49
  flowers, 28, 44, 47
  forget-me-nots, 23
  for illusion of sunlight, 31
  leaves, 31, 41
  stamens, 144
piping
  achieving mastery, 304
  Australian style, 9
  basket weave, 158, 159
  to cover cracks and spaces, 52
  freehand (See embroidery techniques, freehand
    piping)
  lace, cornelli, 8, 50, 54
  lattice, 19
  leaves, 25, 39, 158, 159, 161, 163

piping *(continued)*

  overpiping

    lines, 66, 106, 108–109

    scrollwork, 106, 108–110

  petal blossoms, 22–24

  rope, 88

  rosettes, 26, 158, 159

  shadow-piping, 73

  snail's trail (bead border; oval border), 52

  "stitches," 117

  stringwork, 50, 52–54, 108, 120, 122–123

  Swiss dots, 20, 21

  types, 3

pizza wheel, 65, 92, 98

plaques. *See also* panels; Pastillage

  monogrammed, 111

  name tag, 95

  pattern, 215

  transferring pattern to, 15

plastic chocolate. *See* modeling chocolate

plastic wrap

  flooding piped onto, 69, 70, 71

  lattice piped onto, 99

plunger flowers

  on cakes, 72, 142, 143

  on cookies, 152, 154

  on cupcakes, 159

  technique, 10–11

practice. *See* mastery, achieving

presses. *See* molds and presses

pumpkin, cake, 132, 134–137

Q

Quick Gumpaste, 200

quilting wheel

  to score a guideline, 52

  stitched effect, 62, 63, 79, 81, 115, 116, 130

R

recipes, 165–203

  Apricot Jam, Sieved, 203

  cake

    Banana-Rum, 175

    Cream Cheese Pound, 174

    Devil's Food, 170

    Lemon Cream Pound, 168

    Orange Cream Pound, 167

    Silver White, 169

    Simnel, 172–173

    Traditional Pound, 166

    Victoria Sponge, 171

  cookies

    Almond Paste, 181

    Butter, 179

    Chocolate, 182

    Lemon or Orange Cream, 180

  cupcake

    Almond Paste, 176

    Chocolate Fudge, 177

    Yellow Cake, 178

  Curd, Lemon, Lime, or Orange, 202

  customization of, 5

  Ganache, 186

  Glaze, Confectioners' (Gum Glue), 194

  Gumpaste, Quick, 200

  icing

    Almond-Vanilla Buttercream, 189

    Coconut-Rum Buttercream, 190

    Dark Chocolate Buttercream, 187

    Decorator's Buttercream, 191

    Egg White Royal, 198

    Flood, 201

    French Vanilla Buttercream, 192

    how to thin, 17, 21, 25

    Italian Meringue Buttercream, 188

    Lemon-Infused Buttercream, 184–185

    Lime-Infused Buttercream, 185

    Meringue Powder Royal, 199

    Orange-Infused Buttercream, 185

    Swiss Meringue Buttercream, 193

  Marzipan, 195

modeling chocolate
    Chocolate Plastic, 196
    Dark, 196
    White, 196
    White, Paste, 197
    Pastillage, 183
ribbon
    fabric
        attached to decorations, 55, 146–147
        border, 140, 152
        to finish stringwork, 54
    gumpaste
        streamers, 112, 118–119
        two-layered, 74, 79–81, 126, 130
        two-toned, 58, 62–63
rolling pin
    to roll out gumpaste, 29, 40, 64
    textured, 65, 116
rope
    gumpaste, 15, 115, 119
    modeling chocolate, 162, 163
    piped, 88
rosettes, piped, 26, 158, 159
Round Chocolate Fan Cookie and Upright Heart-
    Shaped Cookie, 154–155
runout (flooding technique), 17–18

S

sandpaper, 87, 92, 98, 144
scallop design
    creating template for, 52
    pattern, 218
    piped, 8, 106–111
scissors, 21, 49, 144
scrollwork, 106, 108–110
seasonal cakes, 25, 31, 124–147
Season's Greetings, 126–131
shine
    creation on gumpaste, 31, 41, 64
    creation on marzipan, 161, 163
    from gum glue, 194
shortening, high-ratio, 185, 193

Sieved Apricot Jam, 203
Silver White Cake, 169
Simnel Cake, 67, 172–173
skewer, wooden, 98, 99, 144
small bites, cookies and cupcakes, 148–163
The Society of Creative Anachronism, 113
South African technique. See Nirvana Cake; Nirvana
    style
spatula
    metal or metal offset, 18, 21, 53, 161, 163
    rubber, 196, 197
spring designs, 140–147
Spring Love, 140–147
squeeze bottle, 17, 18
stickpin
    to mark guidelines, 108, 110, 122
    to secure templates, 52
    to transfer patterns, 15, 38, 76
stitched effect
    piped, 117
    with quilting wheel, 62, 63, 79, 81, 115, 116, 130
storage
    curd, 202
    edible flowers, 10, 21
    gumpaste, 26, 29, 200
    icing, 198, 201
    marzipan, 195
    modeling chocolate, 196
stringwork. See piping, stringwork
Styrofoam, base of drying rack, 27, 29, 31, 41, 49, 62
sweet peas, royal icing, 24
Swiss dots, 20, 21
Swiss Meringue Buttercream, 193

T

tape
    florist
        African daisy, 47
        chincherinchee, 49
        spiral foliage, 31
        spray of berries, 41, 131

tape *(continued)*
  masking
    to secure patterns, 15, 18, 38
    to secure templates, 52
tassels, 14, 115
techniques, basic, 15–16, 38–39
templates. *See* patterns
texture
  bubble wrap, 58, 63, 65
  corn cob, 137, 139
  embossing, 65, 116, 137, 155 (*See also* grater;
    rolling pin, textured)
  lace, 155
  leaf, 31, 137 (*See also* molds and presses, leaf)
  orange peel, 161
Textured Iced Cookie, 155
tiers, 35
Tiffany-Inspired Ribbon Cake, 74–81, 208
tip space, 158
toothpick
  as a marker, 122
  to sculpt marzipan, 161
  to spread flood icing, 17, 18
Traditional Pound Cake, 166
transfer techniques. *See also* patterns
  for brush embroidery, 15, 38
  carbon copy method, 15, 76, 111
  for flooded panels, 69, 70, 71
  for freehand embroidery, 9–10
  stickpin, 15, 38, 76
tray, artist, 28, 31, 76
trellis work. *See* drop strings
trumpet, 27, 144
tulips, brush embroidery, 36, 37–38

V

vegetables, gumpaste, 132–139
Venetian Mask Cake, 84–89, 209
Victorian style
  birthday cakes, 57
  characteristics, 1
  tassels, 14
  wedding cakes, 105, 107

Victoria Sponge Cake, 171
violets, royal icing, 23–24

W

Wagner Spray gun, 87
water
  to clean brushes, 76, 142
  to dilute gel food colors, 76
  to thin icing, 17, 21, 25
wedding cakes, 104–123
wedding favors, 83, 149
White Modeling Chocolate, 196
White Modeling Chocolate Paste, 197
whitener, liquid, 76, 142, 143
wire
  to display
    berries, 40, 41, 47, 131
    blossoms, 27, 44, 47, 48, 49
    leaves, 29, 30, 40–41
    stamens, 144
  to guide gumpaste, 62, 64
  to secure stamens, 144
  spiral foliage, 30, 31, 95
  spiral heart, 140, 146–147
writing. *See* calligraphy

X

X-acto knife
  to cut decoration from clay gun, 14, 15
  to cut out a pattern, 64, 86, 98, 111, 116, 134
  to cut out a shape, 11, 79, 80, 130, 137, 138
  scores to create a blossom, 27, 144
  scores to create texture, 137
  to trim, 18, 80, 92, 101

Y

Yellow Cake Cupcakes, 178